## Celebrate *Country Woman Christmas 2000*

Festive lights twinkling from rooftops…farmsteads blanketed in snow…little children hanging stockings with care…plates of cookies fresh from the oven—these bright sights can mean only one thing. It's Christmastime!

There isn't any other holiday quite like it. To help you celebrate Noel to the very fullest, we've again bundled the best this season has to offer into this fifth annual edition of *Country Woman Christmas*.

It's chock-full of heartwarming stories, recipes, crafts and photos, all with a *country* focus. That's because much of this book comes directly from the readers of *Country Woman* magazine. Here's a peek at what's waiting for you inside…

Delectable Delights. An abundance of goodies, from appetizers to sweets, breakfast dishes, dinner fixin's and more, flavor this keepsake publication's pages. With over *100* never-before-published recipes at your fingertips, your holiday table is sure to impress.

These aren't just any recipes, though. Each dish had to pass rigorous tests in the *Country Woman* kitchen—plus an equally important *time* test. During the hustle and bustle of the holidays, busy country cooks like you don't have much extra time to make trips in to town. That's why every recipe in this book can be made with ingredients you likely already have on hand in your pantry.

Fast Crafts. You'll find dozens of original holiday craft projects within these pages, too. Each comes complete with instructions, patterns and charts and takes no more than a few hours to finish. But they'll all lend merriment to your home during December…and beyond.

You'll also enjoy reading about country women who create their own unique brand of Christmas cheer and learning their special tricks for bringing the holidays home.

Plus, you can explore fun ways to decorate your home with festive flair, read true stories about the joy of Christmas and smile at our other merry features and photos.

More in Store. With a colorful new edition being added to this series every year, you can look forward to many more country-flavored holiday celebrations. But, for now, simply settle back with *Country Woman Christmas 2000*. We hope you enjoy it as much as we've enjoyed bringing it to you!

Executive Editor
Kathy Pohl

Editor
Kathleen Anderson

Food Editor
Janaan Cunningham

Associate Food Editor
Corinne Willkomm

Senior Recipe Editor
Sue A. Jurack

Test Kitchen Assistant
Suzanne Hampton

Craft Editors
Jane Craig
Tricia Coogan

Associate Editors
Sharon Selz
Lori Hurst
Julie Kastello
Michelle Bretl
Kristine Krueger
Jean Steiner

Editorial Assistant
Joanne Wied

Art Directors
Maribeth Greinke
Niki Malmberg

Art Associates
Claudia Wardius
Tom Hunt
Vicky Marie Moseley
Linda Dzik
Bonnie Ziolecki

Photographer
Dan Roberts

Food Photography Artist
Stephanie Marchese

Photo Studio Manager
Anne Schimmel

Production Assistant
Ellen Lloyd

© 2000 Reiman Publications, LLC
5400 S. 60th Street
Greendale WI 53129

International Standard
Book Number:
0-89821-290-1
International Standard
Serial Number:
1093-6750

INSIDE...

AND MUCH MORE!

PICTURED ON OUR COVER. Clockwise from top right: Fun Foam Trimmers (p. 64), Plaid Santa (p. 68), Grandma's Butterscotch Candy (p. 37), Gingerbread Ornaments (p. 96), Christmas Eve Mice (p. 37), Candy Characters (p. 103), Festive Decorated Basket (p. 74), Cowboy Cookie Mix (p. 45).

Photo Contributors: pp. 8-9, Chuck Warner; p. 50, Stephen Michal Photography and Design; pp. 52-54, Joseph Rey Au; p. 57, John Leach, Tony Lotven, Lynda Smith; p. 105, Linda McLaren/LTM Photo; p. 106, Kate Johnson, Mark Harper/Northern Lights Photo Studio; p. 107, Marty Begg, Susan Peebles; p. 109, Mike Nagy, Lynn Stewart; p. 111, Dean Vorhees Studio.

Christmas Eve Journey

I'd love to catch a ride tonight
With Santa on his sleigh,
And journey to a country place
So very far away.

A red brick house high on a hill,
Its rooftop white with snow,
And in the cold December night,
Its windows softly glow.

A tree stands tall beside the fire,
Its perfume scents the air,
Green branches dressed with memories,
Each made with greatest care.

And from his Bible Daddy reads,
While carols softly play,
The greatest story ever told,
Of that first Christmas Day.

The little ones with shining eyes
Hang stockings made of red,
Then Mother listens to their prayers
And tucks them into bed.

I'll be there as the Christmas snow
Paints everything in white,
I'll journey to that country home
In my sweet dreams tonight.

—*Dawn E. McCormick*
Spring, Texas

This Ranch Wife's Santas Are Tailor-Made for the Holidays!

IN the crafty hands of Gloria Clay, Santa is quite the character…a lot of different characters, that is!

"When I think of Kris Kringle, it's not only the familiar red-suited fellow residing in the North Pole that comes to mind," this busy ranch wife and mother of three grown children reveals.

"I also envision him clad in rugged Western duds roaming the range…or wearing traditional Belgian finery in a snow-covered village."

Those out-of-the-ordinary traits—and more—are what Gloria gives the original Claus dolls she creates at her homestead near Laramie, Wyoming.

"I dress them head to toe in historical old-world and American Santa costumes," she says. "I stitch the garments for the mostly 16- and 18-inch figures myself, trying to make them as authentic as possible.

"Each body, also handmade and mounted on a base, is a wood and wire armature I cover with cotton batting, muslin and a clay head. Toys and other accessories I collect for embellishments complete the designs."

Cowboys clothed in blue jeans, leather chaps and sterling silver belt buckles display bridles and Gloria's hand-tooled saddles. Mountaineers also have a hardy look, with fringed vests Gloria beads in Native American motifs and snowshoes she shapes from wood caning and sinew.

Russian Santas with embroidered wool coats and pet polar bears, as well as Father Christmases adorned in rich velvet robes, are also among her creations.

"Besides being a doll-maker, I've long been a bronze sculptor and painter," Gloria notes. "But my St. Nicks are so fun to fashion and share, I haven't stopped assembling them since I first gave a few as gifts several years ago."

Finding time in her schedule can be challenging, Gloria admits, on the ranch she operates with husband Perry, son Jim, daughter-in-law Maggie and grandsons Trampis and Brogan.

"I'm often running cattle, cutting hay or even staying up nights for 2 months straight during calving," Gloria relates. "But fitting my crafting into spare moments is worthwhile.

"Folks who have my Santas in their homes often tell me they don't put them away after December 25. They leave them out from holiday to holiday—so I like to think my dolls help extend the spirit of Christmas all year long."

Editor's Note: *For more details on Gloria's Santas, contact her at 423 State Hwy. 11, Laramie WY 82070; 1-307/745-7959.* ☆

GO FIGURE—that's what Gloria Clay (at top right) does merrily when she creates St. Nicks in all shapes and sizes.

WELCOME TO MY COUNTRY KITCHEN

By Glenda Watkins of Fairmont, West Virginia

CHRISTMAS might come and go in other kitchens, but the heart of our country home always features a colorful festive glow!

Since I've long delighted in December 25, it seemed reasonable to season the kitchen with Yuletide flair after we moved into our new home several years back. Happily, my husband, Eugene, agreed…and together we've created a merry space that suits us all year-round.

That's not to say I don't do any decking during December—we both relish wrapping the room in Noel novelties and bringing our happy style full circle.

In Step with Christmas

Grounding our surroundings in good cheer is the wall-to-wall carpeting we installed. Colorfully covered in pine boughs and poinsettias, it creates a festive tone as soon as visitors set foot inside the door.

Lacy crimson curtains covering the back door window and the panes above the sink outline the look. So do other everyday objects, like the perky red pitcher atop the refrigerator, a strawberry-trimmed cookie jar brightening the shelf above the oven and a lively grouping of canisters with red covers accenting the white-flecked counters.

Those spacious easy-to-clean counters come in handy when I'm in the midst of baking batches of yummy Christmas cookies and other mouth-watering treats for friendly get-togethers and delicious gift-giving.

The winding ivy stencil that tops the white walls on one side of the room and gracefully borders the light switch near the kitchen fits fine into our festive approach as well.

Complementing the appealing strand of greenery are whimsical pictures framed in holiday hues. The playful pair features nostalgic scenes that capture the character of our kitchen. Their simple country charm creates a feeling of family and warmth that never goes out of style.

To further enhance the area, I add artificial holly garlands studded with twinkling lights. The verdant trim twines along the upper edges of the pine cabinets and acts as a lively fore-ground for a charming assortment of roosters, ducks and a simple silver kettle.

Below, glass cabinet doors bear fanciful floral designs that catch the eye during the season and beyond. The doors were originally made of solid wood, but Eugene removed the center panels and replaced them with glass, then I added the artful motifs with liquid leading. The rustic hinges and handles we attached forge extra country appeal.

Every nook and cranny holds holiday cheer. Angels alight on the corner curio cabinets, a Santa dispenses soap at the sink and fabric candy canes sweeten the door.

A stuffed Santa and tall Christmas doll greet guests while a stand of candles highlights the kitchen window. Even the cheery refrigerator magnets make spirits bright.

A Yuletide Setting

The inviting kitchen table completes our joyful Yuletide ensemble. Dinnerware adorned in holly combines with ruby-hued napkins, a wreath of scarlet candles and an old-fashioned tasseled tablecloth to create a warm nostalgic spot, perfect for any size celebration.

We love entertaining, and this kitchen makes everyone feel at home for the holidays. We especially enjoy welcoming our two grown children and our seven grandchildren for yummy Christmas dishes and hearty conversation. And, of

course, the kitchen is a favorite gathering spot.

I can't help but feel happy when we're all enjoying each other's company in here. It really makes me appreciate the simpler things in life.

I hope you enjoyed touring my cozy Noel niche. Happy Holidays!

COOKING UP a Noel look in the kitchen is a favorite task for Glenda Watkins (shown at far left above). She starts with everyday accents, like pine-and-poinsettia carpet and red curtains, then seasons with holly garland, dashing dishes and Christmas characters for a cozy holiday haven flavored with good cheer.

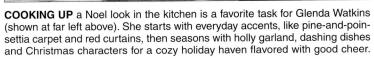

BOUNTIFUL BRUNCH. Shown clockwise from bottom right: Christmas Fruit Kabobs (p. 11), Festive Scrambled Eggs (p. 11) and Almond Apricot Logs (p. 11).

Holiday Brunch

CHRISTMAS FRUIT KABOBS
Lois Rutherford, St. Augustine, Florida
(Pictured on page 10)

My chunky fruit skewers are always a hit for brunch, whether served with pastries, quiche or eggs and bacon. They're also excellent appetizers and potluck additions.

    1/2 fresh pineapple, trimmed and cut into
       1-inch chunks
    4 kiwifruit, peeled and cut into 1-inch pieces
    3 navel oranges, peeled and sectioned
    3 medium apples, cut into 1-inch pieces
    3 medium firm bananas, cut into 1-inch pieces
    1 jar (10 ounces) maraschino cherries, drained
SAUCE:
    1 egg yolk
    1/4 cup maple syrup *or* honey
    2 tablespoons lemon juice
    3/4 cup whipping cream, whipped

Alternately thread fruit onto skewers. Cover and refrigerate until serving. In a saucepan over low heat, cook and stir the egg yolk and syrup until a thermometer reads 160°. Remove from the heat; stir in lemon juice. Cool completely. Fold in the whipped cream. Serve with fruit for dipping. Refrigerate any leftovers. **Yield:** 20 kabobs (about 1 cup sauce).

ALMOND APRICOT LOGS
L. Kniffin, Hockessin, Delaware
(Pictured on page 10)

This is a treat my family insists I make each year for the holidays. We often refer to these sweet bread bites simply as "good things". They're super served warm.

    2 packages (1/4 ounce *each*) active dry yeast
    1/3 cup warm water (110° to 115°)
1-1/2 cups warm milk (110° to 115°)
    1/3 cup vegetable oil
    1/2 cup sugar
    2 eggs
    2 teaspoons salt
    2 teaspoons ground nutmeg
    5 to 5-1/2 cups all-purpose flour
1-1/2 cups coarsely chopped dried apricots
    1 cup chopped almonds
GLAZE:
1-1/2 cups confectioners' sugar
    1/2 teaspoon vanilla extract
    2 to 3 tablespoons milk

In a large mixing bowl, dissolve yeast in water. Add the milk, oil, sugar, eggs, salt, nutmeg and 2 cups flour. Beat until smooth. Add apricots and almonds. Stir in enough remaining flour to form a soft dough. Turn onto a floured surface; knead until smooth and elastic, about 6-8 minutes. Place in a greased bowl, turning once to grease top. Cov-

er and let rise in a warm place until doubled, about 1-1/2 hours. Punch dough down; let rest for 10 minutes. Turn onto a lightly floured surface. Roll into a 15-in. x 12-in. rectangle. Cut into 3-in. x 1-in. strips. Place 1 in. apart on greased baking sheets. Cover and let rise until doubled, about 30 minutes. Bake at 375° for 15 minutes or until light golden brown. Remove to wire racks. For glaze, combine the confectioners' sugar, vanilla and enough milk to achieve desired consistency. Brush over warm logs. **Yield:** 5 dozen.

FESTIVE SCRAMBLED EGGS
Fern Raleigh, Windom, Kansas
(Pictured on page 10)

Every bit as quick as scrambled eggs are meant to be, this hearty dish—with red pimientos and green parsley or chives— is nice for hectic Christmas mornings.

    12 eggs
1-1/3 cups milk, *divided*
    1/2 to 1 teaspoon salt
    1/4 teaspoon pepper
    2 tablespoons diced pimientos
    2 tablespoons minced fresh parsley *or* chives
    2 tablespoons all-purpose flour
    1/4 cup butter *or* margarine

In a large bowl, beat eggs and 1 cup milk. Add the salt, pepper, pimientos and parsley. In a small bowl, combine flour and remaining milk until smooth; stir into egg mixture. In a large skillet, melt butter over medium heat. Add egg mixture. Cook and stir over medium heat until the eggs are completely set. **Yield:** 6 servings.

BACON POPOVERS
Marisa May, Fairport, New York

Even picky youngsters find the eggs and hint of bacon in these popovers irresistible. For delicious variety, try pairing them with maple syrup or cheese sauce.

    2 eggs
    1 cup milk
    1 tablespoon vegetable oil
    1 cup all-purpose flour
    1/4 teaspoon salt
    3 bacon strips, cooked and crumbled

In a mixing bowl, beat the eggs, milk and oil. Beat in flour and salt just until smooth (do not overbeat). Using two 12-cup muffin tins, grease and flour six alternating cups in each pan. Fill ungreased muffins cups two-thirds full with water. Fill greased muffin cups two-thirds full with batter. Sprinkle bacon over batter. Bake at 400° for 25-30 minutes or until puffed and golden. Serve warm. Refrigerate any leftovers. **Yield:** 1 dozen.

SPICED RAISIN MINI MUFFINS
Faye Hintz, Springfield, Missouri

These flavorful moist muffins don't crumble when you bite into them. So you may want to take them into the living room for munching while opening gifts.

 1 cup sugar
 1 cup chopped raisins
 1 cup water
 1/2 cup butter *or* margarine
 1 teaspoon ground cinnamon
 1/2 teaspoon ground cloves
 2 cups all-purpose flour
 1 teaspoon baking soda
 1/2 teaspoon salt
 1 cup chopped walnuts
GLAZE:
 1 cup confectioners' sugar
 1/2 teaspoon vanilla extract
 1 to 2 tablespoons milk

In a saucepan, combine the first six ingredients. Bring to a boil over medium heat, stirring occasionally. Remove from the heat; cool to room temperature. In a bowl, combine the flour, baking soda and salt. Add raisin mixture; mix well. Stir in walnuts. Fill greased or paper-lined miniature muffin cups two-thirds full. Bake at 350° for 12-16 minutes or until a toothpick comes out clean. Cool for 5 minutes before removing from pans to wire racks. For glaze, combine the confectioners' sugar, vanilla and enough milk to achieve desired consistency. Drizzle over cooled muffins. **Yield:** about 4-1/2 dozen.

RAISIN PINWHEEL LOAF
Jackie van Trigt, New Hamburg, Ontario

These slices are always welcome Christmas morning, especially when they're paired with steaming cups of coffee or tea. I've doubled and even quadrupled the recipe many times.

 1 cup raisins
 1/2 cup ground almonds
 1/4 cup sugar
 2 egg whites
 1/8 teaspoon almond extract
DOUGH:
 2 cups all-purpose flour
 2 teaspoons baking powder
 1/2 teaspoon salt
 1/2 cup cold butter *or* margarine
 1/2 cup milk
 1/4 cup sugar
 2 egg yolks
 2 teaspoons grated lemon peel
Half-and-half cream
Additional sugar
GLAZE:
 1 cup confectioners' sugar
 2 tablespoons milk

For filling, combine the first five ingredients in a bowl; set aside. In a large bowl, combine the flour, baking powder and salt. Cut in butter until the mixture resembles coarse

crumbs. Add milk, sugar, egg yolks and lemon peel; mix well. Turn onto a floured surface; knead 12 times. Roll into a 12-in. x 8-in. rectangle. Spread filling to within 1 in. of edges. Roll up, jelly-roll style, starting with a long side; pinch seams to seal and tuck ends under. Place, seam side down, on a greased baking sheet. Brush dough with cream and sprinkle with additional sugar. Bake at 375° for 40-45 minutes or until golden brown (top will crack). Remove to a wire rack. Combine glaze ingredients; drizzle over warm bread. To serve, cut into 1-in. slices. **Yield:** 12 servings.

APPLE-CHEDDAR FRENCH TOAST
Lila Hadaway, Polo, Illinois

Plentiful layers of bread, ham, pie filling and more in this sweet-savory dish remind me of lasagna—only for breakfast. I lost count long ago of the number of recipe requests I've received.

 2 packages (12-1/2 ounces *each*) frozen
  French toast
 8 ounces thinly sliced fully cooked ham
2-1/2 cups (10 ounces) shredded cheddar
  cheese, *divided*
 1 can (21 ounces) apple pie filling
 1 cup granola cereal with raisins
 1 cup (8 ounces) sour cream
 1/3 cup packed brown sugar

Prepare French toast according to package directions. Place six slices in an ungreased 13-in. x 9-in. x 2-in. baking dish. Top with ham, 2 cups cheese and remaining French toast. Spread pie filling over top; sprinkle with granola. Bake, uncovered, at 350° for 25 minutes. Sprinkle with remaining cheese; bake 5 minutes longer or until cheese is melted. In a bowl, combine sour cream and brown sugar; serve with French toast. Refrigerate leftovers. **Yield:** 6-8 servings.

CHRISTMAS BRUNCH CASSEROLE
Mary Eckler, Louisville, Kentucky

No one leaves the table hungry when I serve this savory casserole. In fact, folks rave about it! What I like as much as the taste is that I can prepare it ahead of time.

 2 pounds bulk pork sausage
 1 large onion, chopped
 2 cups cooked rice
 3 cups crisp rice cereal
 3 cups (12 ounces) shredded cheddar cheese
 6 eggs
 2 cans (10-3/4 ounces *each*) condensed cream of
  celery soup, undiluted
 1/2 cup milk

In a skillet, cook sausage and onion over medium heat until meat is no longer pink; drain. Place in a lightly greased 13-in. x 9-in. x 2-in. baking dish. Layer with the rice, cereal and cheddar cheese. In a bowl, beat the eggs, soup and milk. Spread over top. Bake, uncovered, at 350° for 55-60 minutes or until a knife inserted near the center comes out clean. Let stand for 5 minutes before cutting. Refrigerate any leftovers. **Yield:** 12 servings.

HAM AND EGGS TART
Marge Scardino, Milwaukee, Wisconsin

This hearty tart ensures a good hot breakfast with a minimum of fuss. It's so versatile that you can add different toppings, such as chopped olives and Monterey Jack cheese.

    1/4 cup chopped onion
      1 tablespoon butter *or* margarine
      1 cup cubed fully cooked ham
      1 tube (8 ounces) refrigerated crescent rolls
      4 eggs
    1/2 cup milk
    1/2 teaspoon salt
    1/4 teaspoon pepper
      1 cup (4 ounces) shredded Swiss cheese
      1 tablespoon minced chives

In a skillet, saute onion in butter until tender. Remove from the heat; stir in ham and set aside. Unroll crescent roll dough into one long rectangle. Press onto the bottom and 1 in. up the sides of a greased 13-in. x 9-in. x 2-in. baking dish; seal seams and perforations. Spread with reserved ham mixture. In a bowl, beat eggs, milk, salt and pepper; stir in cheese. Pour over ham. Sprinkle with chives. Bake at 375° for 23-28 minutes or until a knife inserted in center comes out clean. Refrigerate leftovers. **Yield: 8-10 servings.**

ALMOND-TOPPED SPICED PEACHES
Beverly Rogers, Orange, California

A dab of cinnamon-flavored sour cream is the perfect complement to these nutty curried peaches. In the oven, the fruit juice forms a wonderful sauce for spooning over each serving.

      2 cans (*29 ounces each*) peach halves, drained
    1/2 cup packed brown sugar
    1/4 cup butter *or* margarine
    1/2 to 1 teaspoon curry powder
    1/4 cup sliced almonds
      1 cup (8 ounces) sour cream
      1 teaspoon ground cinnamon

Place peach halves in an ungreased shallow 2-qt. baking dish; set aside. In a saucepan, combine the brown sugar, butter and curry powder. Cook and stir over low heat until sugar is dissolved. Pour over peaches. Sprinkle with almonds. Bake, uncovered, at 375° for 20 minutes or until heated through. Combine sour cream and cinnamon; serve with peaches. **Yield: 6-8 servings.**

PLUM SAUSAGE BITES
Heidi Fisher, Victoria, British Columbia

Packed with perky flavor and a thick sauce that clings to the sausage, these links are a must for my brunches and potlucks. Plus, the recipe couldn't be much simpler to make.

      2 to 2-1/2 pounds uncooked pork sausage links,
        cut into 1-inch pieces
      1 cup plum, apple *or* grape jelly

      2 tablespoons soy sauce
      1 tablespoon Dijon mustard

In a large skillet, cook sausage over medium heat until no longer pink; drain and set sausage aside. In the same skillet, combine the jelly, soy sauce and mustard; mix well. Simmer, uncovered, for 5 minutes, stirring occasionally. Return sausage to the pan and heat through. Refrigerate any leftovers. **Yield: 18-22 servings.**

FRUIT-TOPPED BUTTERMILK PANCAKES
Arlene Butler, Ogden, Utah

Years of trying different pancake recipes hasn't changed my opinion that this classic one is best. A generous dollop of warm fruit on top makes the meal truly special.

      1 package (10 ounces) frozen sweetened
        raspberries, thawed
      2 medium ripe bananas, sliced
      1 can (8 ounces) pineapple chunks, drained
    1/2 cup packed brown sugar
PANCAKES:
1-3/4 cups all-purpose flour
      2 tablespoons sugar
      2 teaspoons baking powder
      1 teaspoon baking soda
    1/2 teaspoon salt
      2 eggs
      2 cups buttermilk
    1/4 cup vegetable oil
    1/2 teaspoon vanilla extract

In a blender, combine raspberries, bananas, pineapple and brown sugar; cover and process until blended. Transfer to a small saucepan; cook and stir over low heat until heated through. Set aside and keep warm. For pancakes, combine the dry ingredients in a bowl. In another bowl, beat the eggs, buttermilk, oil and vanilla. Stir into dry ingredients just until moistened. Pour batter by 1/4 cupfuls onto a greased hot griddle. Turn when bubbles form on top; cook until the second side is golden brown. Serve with warm fruit topping. **Yield: about 1-1/2 dozen pancakes (2-1/2 cups topping).**

MAPLE BUTTER
Kathy Scott, Hemingford, Nebraska

It's easy to add maple flavor to the breakfast table with this rich spread. Slather the butter on piping-hot pancakes, waffles and toast—your family will love it!

    1/2 cup butter (no substitutes), softened
    1/2 cup sugar
    1/2 teaspoon vanilla extract
    1/2 teaspoon maple flavoring

In a mixing bowl, cream butter, sugar, vanilla and maple flavoring until smooth. Spread over toast, waffles and pancakes. Cover and refrigerate until ready to serve. **Yield: about 1 cup.**

Christmas Breads

VERY CHERRY CRESCENT RING
Karen Sevensky, Hackettstown, New Jersey
(Pictured on page 16)

My mother used to prepare this pretty coffee cake on Christmas Eve for our family to enjoy the next morning after opening gifts. It's an easy way to add an elegant touch to a holiday breakfast or brunch.

    1 jar (10 ounces) maraschino cherries, drained
    1 package (8 ounces) cream cheese, softened
1/2 cup sugar
1/2 teaspoon almond extract
3/4 cup chopped pecans
    2 tubes (8 ounces *each*) refrigerated crescent rolls
GLAZE:
    1 cup confectioners' sugar
    4 teaspoons milk
1/4 teaspoon almond extract
  10 pecan halves

Set aside five cherries for garnish. Chop remaining cherries; place in a mixing bowl. Add cream cheese, sugar, almond extract and pecans; beat until blended. Unroll crescent roll dough. Place dough together, forming one large rectangle; seal seams and perforations. Fold dough in half lengthwise; roll into an 18-in. x 12-in. rectangle. Spread filling to within 1 in. of edges. Roll up tightly, jelly-roll style, starting with a long side; pinch seam to seal. Place seam side down on a greased baking sheet; pinch ends together to form a ring. With a scissors, cut from outside edge two-thirds of the way toward center of the ring at 1-in. intervals. Separate strips slightly; twist to allow filling to show, slightly overlapping previous piece. Bake at 375° for 20-30 minutes or until golden brown. Cover loosely with foil if the top browns too quickly. Using two large spatulas, carefully remove to a wire rack. For glaze, combine confectioners' sugar, milk and almond extract. Drizzle over warm ring. Garnish with pecans and reserved cherries. **Yield:** 1 loaf.

CRANBERRY SWEET POTATO BREAD
Margaret Pache, Mesa, Arizona
(Pictured on page 17)

We grow plenty of sweet potatoes, so I try to use them in different ways. Slices of this bread, studded with dried cranberries and nuts, are especially tasty served with the citrusy cream cheese spread.

    1 cup orange juice
1/2 cup dried cranberries
    1 package (8 ounces) cream cheese, softened
    3 tablespoons confectioners' sugar
    1 teaspoon lemon extract
DOUGH:
1/3 cup butter *or* margarine, softened
1-1/4 cups sugar

    1 egg
    1 cup cold mashed sweet potatoes
1-3/4 cups all-purpose flour
    1 teaspoon ground cinnamon
1/2 teaspoon baking powder
1/2 teaspoon baking soda
1/2 teaspoon salt
1/2 cup dried cranberries
1/2 cup chopped macadamia nuts *or* almonds

In a saucepan, combine orange juice and cranberries; bring to a boil. Reduce heat. Simmer, uncovered, for 5 minutes or until cranberries are softened; drain. In a mixing bowl, beat cream cheese, confectioners' sugar and lemon extract until smooth. Fold in cranberry mixture. Cover and refrigerate for at least 1 hour. Meanwhile, in a mixing bowl, cream butter and sugar. Beat in egg and sweet potatoes. Combine the dry ingredients; gradually add to creamed mixture. Fold in cranberries and nuts. Transfer to a greased 9-in. x 5-in. x 3-in. loaf pan. Bake at 350° for 55-65 minutes or until a toothpick comes out clean. Cover loosely with foil if the top browns too quickly. Cool for 10 minutes before removing from pan to a wire rack. Serve with the cream cheese spread. **Yield:** 1 loaf.

SWEDISH CINNAMON TWISTS
Cherie Baker, Whitetail, Montana
(Pictured on page 16)

These tender twists are fantastic with fresh-brewed coffee. Although the recipe makes a big batch, the treats never seem to last long at our house.

    2 packages (1/4 ounce *each*) active dry yeast
1/2 cup warm water (110° to 115°)
    2 cups warm buttermilk* (110° to 115°)
1/2 cup butter *or* margarine, softened
    6 tablespoons sugar
    2 eggs
    2 teaspoons salt
1/2 teaspoon baking soda
7-1/2 cups all-purpose flour
FILLING:
1/4 cup butter *or* margarine, melted
    1 cup packed brown sugar
    1 teaspoon ground cinnamon
GLAZE:
    1 cup confectioners' sugar
    1 tablespoon butter *or* margarine, melted
    1 tablespoon hot water

In a mixing bowl, dissolve yeast in warm water. Add the buttermilk, butter, sugar, eggs, salt and baking soda; mix well. Stir in flour to form a soft dough. Turn onto a floured surface; knead until smooth and elastic, about 6-8 minutes. Place in a greased bowl, turning once to grease top. Cover and let rise in a warm place until doubled, about 1-1/2 hours. Punch dough down. Turn onto a lightly floured surface; divide in half. Roll each into a 16-in. x 9-in. rectangle; brush with butter. Combine brown sugar and cinnamon; sprinkle over dough. Fold in half lengthwise, forming a 16-in. x 4-1/2-in. rectangle; pinch edges to seal. Cut into 4-1/2-in. x 1-in. strips; twist each strip two or three times. Place 2 in. apart on greased baking sheets. Cover and let rise until doubled, about 30 minutes. Bake at 375° for 12-14 minutes or until golden brown. Remove from pans to wire racks to cool. Combine glaze ingredients; spoon over warm twists. **Yield:** 2-1/2 to 3 dozen. ***Editor's Note:** Warmed buttermilk will appear curdled.

SOFT YEAST PAN ROLLS
Angie Price, Bradford, Tennessee
(Pictured on page 17)

Want to do something special for a good friend or neighbor? Bake them a pan of these melt-in-your-mouth rolls!

> 2 packages (1/4 ounce *each*) active dry yeast
> 1 teaspoon plus 2/3 cup sugar, *divided*
> 1 cup warm water (110° to 115°)
> 1/2 cup butter *or* margarine, softened
> 1/2 cup shortening
> 1 teaspoon salt
> 1 cup boiling water
> 2 eggs
> 7 to 7-1/2 cups all-purpose flour

In a bowl, dissolve yeast and 1 teaspoon sugar in warm water; let stand for 5 minutes. In a mixing bowl, cream butter, shortening, salt and remaining sugar. Add boiling water; cool to 110°-115°. Add yeast mixture and eggs; mix well. Stir in enough flour to form a soft dough. Turn onto a floured surface; knead until smooth and elastic, about 6-8 minutes. Place in a greased bowl, turning once to grease top. Cover and let rise in a warm place until doubled, about 1 hour. Punch dough down. Turn onto a lightly floured surface; divide into thirds. Divide each portion into nine pieces; shape into balls. Place in three greased 9-in. round baking pans. Cover and let rise until doubled, about 30 minutes. Bake at 350° for 20-25 minutes or until golden brown. Cool in pans on wire racks. **Yield:** 27 rolls.

PUMPKIN SURPRISE MUFFINS
Elizabeth Blondefield, San Jose, California
(Pictured on page 17)

Filled with cream cheese and apricot preserves, these almond-topped pumpkin muffins are heavenly.

> 2 cups all-purpose flour
> 1/2 cup plus 3 tablespoons sugar, *divided*
> 3 teaspoons baking powder
> 1 teaspoon ground cinnamon
> 1/4 teaspoon salt
> 1/4 teaspoon ground nutmeg
> 1/4 teaspoon ground ginger
> 2 eggs
> 1 cup cooked *or* canned pumpkin
> 1/2 cup sour cream
> 6 tablespoons butter *or* margarine, melted
> 6 tablespoons apricot preserves, *divided*

> 1 package (3 ounces) cream cheese, cut into
> 12 cubes
> 1/4 cup sliced almonds

In a bowl, combine the flour, 1/2 cup sugar, baking powder, cinnamon, salt, nutmeg and ginger. In another bowl, beat the eggs, pumpkin, sour cream, butter and 3 tablespoons preserves. Stir into the dry ingredients just until moistened. Fill greased or paper-lined muffin cups half full. Place a cream cheese cube and 3/4 teaspoon of preserves in each. Top with remaining batter. Sprinkle with almonds and remaining sugar. Bake at 400° for 20-25 minutes or until a toothpick comes out clean. Cool for 5 minutes before removing from pan to a wire rack. **Yield:** 1 dozen.

HERBED-TOMATO CHEESE BREAD
Sheila Kimball, Simcoe, Ontario
(Pictured below)

This rustic-looking loaf is so versatile. Thick slices are great with Sunday breakfast omelets, a salad lunch, a pasta dinner…or even as an appetizer for guests.

> 3 cups all-purpose flour
> 1/2 cup grated Parmesan cheese
> 1/2 cup crumbled blue cheese
> 2 teaspoons baking powder
> 1 teaspoon baking soda
> 1 teaspoon *each* dried basil, thyme and rosemary, crushed
> 1/2 teaspoon salt
> 1/2 teaspoon pepper
> 1 egg
> 1-1/2 cups buttermilk
> 1/4 cup vegetable oil
> 3 tablespoons tomato paste

In a bowl, combine the flour, cheeses, baking powder, baking soda and seasonings. In another bowl, beat the egg, buttermilk, oil and tomato paste. Stir into dry ingredients just until moistened. Transfer to a greased 8-in. x 4-in. x 2-in. loaf pan. Bake at 350° for 50-55 minutes or until a toothpick comes out clean. Cool for 10 minutes before removing from pan to a wire rack. **Yield:** 1 loaf.

FESTIVE BREADS. Shown clockwise from top left: Swedish Cinnamon Twists (p. 14), Soft Yeast Pan Rolls (p. 15), Cranberry Sweet Potato Bread (p. 14), Pumpkin Surprise Muffins (p. 15) and Very Cherry Crescent Ring (p. 14).

COCONUT BANANA BREAD
Elaine Kyle, Cleveland, Texas

White chocolate is the wonderfully different addition to this tropical-tasting bread. The moist slices are so scrumptious, they disappear as soon as I serve them.

    1 cup butter *or* margarine, melted
1-1/2 cups sugar
    2 eggs
    1 teaspoon vanilla extract
    1 teaspoon rum extract
    2 cups mashed ripe bananas (about 4 medium)
2-3/4 cups all-purpose flour
1-1/4 teaspoons baking soda
    1/2 teaspoon salt
    6 squares (1 ounce *each*) white baking chocolate, coarsely chopped
    1 cup flaked coconut
    1 cup chopped pecans

In a mixing bowl, combine butter and sugar; mix well. Add eggs and extracts; beat on high speed until thickened. Stir in bananas. Combine the flour, baking soda and salt; gradually add to banana mixture. Fold in the chocolate, coconut and pecans. Transfer to two greased 8-in. x 4-in. x 2-in. loaf pans. Bake at 350° for 70-75 minutes or until a toothpick comes out clean. Cool for 10 minutes before removing from pans to wire racks. **Yield:** 2 loaves.

CRANBERRY SCONES
Anne DaCosta, Chambersburg, Pennsylvania

I bake these simple fruit-filled scones during the holidays or any time our children come home for a visit. We all agree there's nothing better for breakfast than these scones, spread with homemade cranberry-orange butter.

1-1/2 cups butter (no substitutes), softened
    1/2 cup fresh *or* frozen cranberries
    2 tablespoons confectioners' sugar
    1/2 teaspoon grated orange peel
SCONES:
2-1/2 cups all-purpose flour
    2/3 cup sugar
2-1/2 teaspoons baking powder
    1/2 teaspoon baking soda
    3/4 cup cold butter (no substitutes)
    1 cup chopped fresh *or* frozen cranberries*
    3/4 cup buttermilk

In a mixing bowl, cream butter. Stir in cranberries, confectioners' sugar and orange peel; mix well. Cover and refrigerate for at least 1 hour. Meanwhile, combine the dry ingredients in a bowl. Cut in butter until mixture resembles coarse crumbs. Add cranberries. Stir in buttermilk just until moistened. Turn onto a lightly floured surface; gently knead 6-8 times. Divide in half. Pat each into an 8-in. circle. Cut into eight wedges. Place 1 in. apart on ungreased baking sheets. Bake at 400° for 15-18 minutes or until lightly browned. Remove from pans to wire racks. Serve warm with cranberry-orange butter. **Yield:** 16 scones. ***Editor's Note:** 3/4 cup dried cranberries may be substituted for the fresh or frozen cranberries.

LEMON BUNS
Betty Peters, Saskatoon, Saskatchewan

These sweet lemony rolls are always a hit no matter where I take them. I enjoy baking—especially with yeast—and this is one of my favorite recipes.

    1 package (2.9 ounces) cook-and-serve lemon pudding/pie filling mix
    2 packages (1/4 ounce *each*) active dry yeast
    2 teaspoons plus 3/4 cup sugar, *divided*
    1 cup warm water (110° to 115°)
    4 eggs, *separated*
    1 cup warm milk (110° to 115°)
    1/2 cup butter *or* margarine, softened
    1/2 teaspoon salt
8-1/2 to 9 cups all-purpose flour
GLAZE:
1-1/2 cups confectioners' sugar
    2 teaspoons lemon juice
    2 to 3 tablespoons milk

Prepare pudding mix according to package directions; cover and refrigerate. In a small bowl, dissolve yeast and 2 teaspoons sugar in warm water; let stand for 5 minutes. In a mixing bowl, beat egg yolks and remaining sugar until thickened. Add the yeast mixture, milk, butter, salt, egg whites and 4 cups flour; beat until smooth. Stir in enough remaining flour to form a soft dough. Turn onto a floured surface; knead until smooth and elastic, about 6-8 minutes. Place in a greased bowl, turning once to grease top. Cover and let rise in a warm place until doubled, about 1 hour. Punch dough down. Turn onto a lightly floured surface; divide into 36 pieces. Roll each piece into a ball. Place 2 in. apart on greased baking sheets. With thumb, make a large indentation in center of each ball; stretch to 3-1/2 in. in diameter. Place about 2 teaspoons of pudding in each indentation. Cover and let rise until doubled, about 30 minutes. Bake at 350° for 15-20 minutes or until golden brown. Remove from pans to wire racks. For glaze, combine the confectioners' sugar, lemon juice and enough milk to achieve desired consistency. Drizzle over warm buns. **Yield:** about 3 dozen.

APRICOT CHEESE BREAD
Karen Meehan, Roodhouse, Illinois

I like to make this fruity bread in a bundt pan for special occasions such as Christmas or Easter morning. Cream cheese, apricots and pecans make it a tantalizing treat.

    2 packages (3 ounces *each*) cream cheese, softened
    1/3 cup sugar
    1 egg
    1 tablespoon all-purpose flour
    1 teaspoon grated orange peel
DOUGH:
    1 cup dried apricots
1-1/2 cups warm water
    2 cups all-purpose flour
    1 cup sugar
    2 teaspoons baking powder
    1 teaspoon salt

1/4 teaspoon baking soda
1 egg
1/2 cup orange juice
1/4 cup vegetable oil
1/4 cup water
1/2 cup chopped pecans

In a mixing bowl, beat the cream cheese, sugar, egg, flour and orange peel until smooth; set aside. Soak apricots in warm water for 15 minutes; drain well. Cut apricots into small pieces; set aside. In a large mixing bowl, combine the dry ingredients. In another bowl, beat the egg, orange juice, oil and water. Stir into the dry ingredients just until moistened. Fold in pecans and apricots. Spoon two-thirds of the batter into a greased and floured 10-in. fluted tube pan. Top with cream cheese filling and remaining batter. Bake at 350° for 55-65 minutes or until a toothpick comes out clean. Cool for 10 minutes before removing from pan to a wire rack to cool completely. Wrap in plastic wrap and refrigerate before slicing. **Yield:** 14-16 servings.

PINK CHERRY BREAD
Gail Graham, Laingsburg, Michigan

Guests won't be able to overlook pieces of this delightful quick bread with its festive color. I bake it for all my Christmas parties, and it's always a big hit.

1 jar (10 ounces) maraschino cherries
3 cups all-purpose flour
2 cups sugar
3 teaspoons baking powder
1/2 teaspoon salt
4 eggs
1-1/2 cups coarsely chopped walnuts
1 cup flaked coconut

Drain cherries, reserving juice. Coarsely chop cherries; set cherries and juice aside. In a bowl, combine the dry ingredients. In another bowl, beat eggs and cherry juice. Stir into dry ingredients just until combined. Fold in the walnuts, coconut and cherries. Transfer to two greased 8-in. x 4-in. x 2-in. loaf pans. Bake at 350° for 60-65 minutes or until a toothpick comes out clean. Cool for 10 minutes before removing from pans to wire racks. **Yield:** 2 loaves.

NUTTY CINNAMON ROLLS
Peggy Sue Underhill, Sonora, Kentucky

I've made batches of these rolls to give to the mail carrier for Christmas, to our church music minister for his birthday and for any number of people who needed a pick-me-up. Thick cream cheese frosting is the fast finishing touch.

2 packages (1/4 ounce *each*) active dry yeast
1/4 cup warm water (110° to 115°)
1 cup warm milk (110° to 115°)
1/4 cup butter *or* margarine, melted
1/2 cup sugar
1 egg
1 teaspoon salt
4-1/2 cups all-purpose flour

FILLING:
1 cup chopped walnuts *or* black walnuts
1/2 cup sugar
1 teaspoon ground cinnamon
1/4 cup butter *or* margarine, melted
FROSTING:
6 tablespoons butter *or* margarine, softened
1 package (3 ounces) cream cheese, softened
3-1/2 cups confectioners' sugar
1-1/2 teaspoons milk
1 teaspoon vanilla extract
1/2 cup chopped walnuts *or* black walnuts

In a mixing bowl, dissolve yeast in water. Beat in the milk, butter, sugar, egg and salt until smooth. Gradually add flour. Turn onto a floured surface; knead until smooth and elastic, about 6-8 minutes. Place in a greased bowl, turning once to grease top. Cover and let rise in a warm place until doubled, about 1 hour. For filling, combine walnuts, sugar and cinnamon; set aside. Punch dough down. Turn onto a lightly floured surface. Roll into an 18-in. x 12-in. rectangle; brush with butter. Sprinkle nut mixture to within 1/2 in. of edges. Roll up, jelly-roll style, starting with a long side. Cut into 12 rolls. Place rolls, cut side up, in a greased 13-in. x 9-in. x 2-in. baking pan. Cover and let rise until doubled, about 45 minutes. Bake at 375° for 20-25 minutes or until golden brown. Cool slightly. For frosting, beat butter and cream cheese until smooth. Add confectioners' sugar, milk and vanilla; mix well. Stir in walnuts. Frost rolls. **Yield:** 1 dozen.

OATMEAL MOLASSES BREAD
Carol Minogue, Buffalo, Minnesota

You're sure to notice the distinctive taste of molasses in this pretty brown loaf. It's my favorite "wholesome" bread recipe. Try it toasted or serve slices with coffee for a quick snack during the busy holiday season.

5 to 5-1/2 cups all-purpose flour
1 cup quick-cooking oats
1/2 cup All-Bran
1/3 cup toasted wheat germ
2 packages (1/4 ounce *each*) active dry yeast
1 tablespoon salt
2 cups water
1/2 cup molasses
2 tablespoons butter *or* margarine
Melted butter *or* margarine, optional

In a large mixing bowl, combine 3 cups flour, oats, All-Bran, wheat germ, yeast and salt. In a saucepan, heat the water, molasses and butter to 120°-130°. Add to dry ingredients; beat until smooth. Stir in enough remaining flour to form a soft dough. Turn onto a floured surface; knead until smooth and elastic, about 6-8 minutes. Place in a greased bowl, turning once to grease top. Cover and let rise in a warm place until doubled, about 1 hour. Punch dough down. Turn onto a lightly floured surface; divide in half. Shape into loaves. Place in two greased 9-in. x 5-in. x 3-in. loaf pans. Cover and let rise until doubled, about 45 minutes. Bake at 375° for 35-40 minutes or until golden brown. Remove from pans to wire racks to cool. Brush tops with butter if desired. **Yield:** 2 loaves.

APPEALING APPETIZERS. Shown clockwise from top left: Ricotta Tart (p. 21), Party Chicken Wings (p. 21) and Colorful Shrimp Spread (p. 21).

Appetizers

COLORFUL SHRIMP SPREAD
Irene Smazal, Prineville, Oregon
(Pictured on page 20)

A friend gave me the recipe for this scrumptious shrimp spread topped with mozzarella cheese and veggies. When I take it to a party or potluck, I never bring leftovers home.

   1 package (8 ounces) cream cheese, softened
   1 bottle (12 ounces) cocktail sauce
   1 can (6 ounces) small shrimp, rinsed and drained
     or 1/3 cup small frozen cooked shrimp, thawed
   2 cups (8 ounces) shredded mozzarella cheese
3/4 cup chopped green pepper
   1 medium tomato, chopped
   4 green onions, sliced
Fresh rosemary and cilantro, optional
Assorted crackers

In a mixing bowl, beat cream cheese until smooth. Spread on a 12-in. round serving platter to within 2 in. of edge. In bowl, combine the cocktail sauce and shrimp; spread over the cream cheese. Sprinkle with mozzarella cheese, green pepper, tomato and onions. Garnish with rosemary and cilantro if desired. Serve with crackers. Refrigerate any leftovers. **Yield:** 8-12 servings.

RICOTTA TART
Teri Rasey-Bolf, Cadillac, Michigan
(Pictured on page 20)

Guests will think you fussed when they bite into a wedge of this cheesy tart. It's so simple to make with prepared pie pastry.

   2 eggs
   1 cup ricotta cheese
   1 cup (4 ounces) shredded sharp cheddar cheese
   2 tablespoons salsa
1/2 teaspoon salt
1/2 teaspoon pepper
Pastry for a single-crust pie (9 inches)

In a bowl, beat eggs. Add the cheeses, salsa, salt and pepper; mix well. Roll out pastry into a 12-in. circle on a foil-lined baking sheet. Spread with cheese mixture to within 1 in. of edge. Fold edge of pastry over outer edge of filling. Bake at 400° for 22-26 minutes or until golden brown. Let stand for 5 minutes before cutting into wedges. Refrigerate any leftovers. **Yield:** 8-12 servings.

PARTY CHICKEN WINGS
Marian Slattery, Whitewater, Wisconsin
(Pictured on page 20)

These moist wings—marinated overnight in a soy sauce, mustard and brown sugar mixture—are excellent party appetizers. At our house, they're a must for holiday gatherings.

  12 whole chicken wings* (about 2 pounds)
3/4 cup soy sauce
1/4 cup water
1/2 cup packed brown sugar
   1 tablespoon Dijon mustard
   1 teaspoon garlic powder

Cut chicken wings into three sections; discard wing tips. In a bowl, combine the remaining ingredients. Set aside 1/4 cup for basting; cover and refrigerate. Place the wings in a large resealable plastic bag or shallow glass bowl. Pour the remaining marinade over wings; turn to coat. Seal or cover and refrigerate overnight. Drain and discard marinade. Place the wings in a shallow baking pan. Bake, uncovered, at 375° for 1 hour, brushing several times with reserved soy sauce mixture during the last 30 minutes of baking. Refrigerate any leftovers. **Yield:** 2 dozen. *Editor's Note:** 2 pounds of uncooked chicken wing sections may be substituted for the whole chicken wings. Omit the first step of the recipe.

CHEESY ARTICHOKE GARLIC LOAF
Diane Hixon, Niceville, Florida

Even people who don't like artichokes will enjoy slices of this delicious crusty bread. The soft interior is rich with sour cream, three kinds of cheese and other goodies.

   1 loaf (20 inches) French bread,
     halved lengthwise
1/2 cup butter *or* margarine
   6 garlic cloves, minced
   2 tablespoons sesame seeds
1-1/2 cups (12 ounces) sour cream
1/4 cup grated Parmesan cheese
   2 tablespoons minced fresh parsley *or* 2
     teaspoons dried parsley flakes
   2 teaspoons lemon-pepper seasoning
   2 cups (8 ounces) cubed Monterey Jack
     cheese
   1 can (14 ounces) water-packed
     artichoke hearts, drained and chopped
   1 can (2-1/4 ounces) sliced ripe olives,
     drained
   1 cup (4 ounces) shredded cheddar cheese
   1 medium, tomato chopped
Additional parsley

Carefully hollow out top and bottom of bread, leaving 1/4-in. shells; set aside. Cut removed bread into small cubes. In a skillet, melt butter. Add the bread cubes, garlic and sesame seeds; cook and stir until butter is absorbed. Remove from the heat. In a bowl, combine sour cream, Parmesan, parsley, lemon-pepper, Monterey Jack cheese, artichokes, olives and bread mixture. Spoon into bread shells; sprinkle with cheddar cheese. Place on ungreased baking sheets. Bake at 350° for 30 minutes or until heated through. Sprinkle with tomato and additional parsley. Refrigerate any leftovers. **Yield:** 10-12 servings.

FRUITY CRANBERRY PUNCH
Joann Dudgeon, Mendon, Ohio

The women's group from our church has held its Christmas potluck at my home for more than 20 years. I never fail to serve this rich and creamy fruit punch...everyone enjoys it.

    4 cups cranberry juice, chilled
    4 cups pineapple juice, chilled
    2 cups sugar, *divided*
    1 to 2 teaspoons almond extract
1/2 gallon strawberry ice cream, softened
    2 cups whipping cream
    1 liter ginger ale, chilled

In a large punch bowl, combine juices, 1-1/2 cups sugar, almond extract and ice cream. Refrigerate until serving. Just before serving, beat cream in a mixing bowl. Gradually add the remaining sugar, beating until soft peaks form. Whisk gently into chilled juice mixture. Add ginger ale. Refrigerate any leftovers. **Yield:** about 7 quarts.

CRAB ROLL-UPS
Emily Scott Kort, Washington, Michigan

These festive pinwheels are the perfect finger food for the buffet table. Chutney is a wonderful surprise in the flavorful filling. Chock-full of goodies, they won't last long.

    1 package (10 ounces) frozen chopped spinach,
      thawed and squeezed dry
    1 envelope vegetable soup mix
1/2 cup mayonnaise
1/2 cup sour cream
    1 package (8 ounces) imitation crabmeat,
      chopped
    1 package (8 ounces) cream cheese, softened
1/4 cup mango chutney *or* chutney of your choice
1/8 teaspoon garlic powder
1/8 teaspoon onion powder
   12 flour tortillas (8 inches)

In a bowl, combine the spinach, soup mix, mayonnaise and sour cream; cover and refrigerate for 1 hour. In another bowl, combine the crab, cream cheese, chutney, garlic powder and onion powder; cover and refrigerate for 1 hour. Spread the spinach mixture on six tortillas. Spread the crab mixture on remaining tortillas. Place one crab tortilla over each spinach tortilla. Roll up tightly, jelly-roll style, and wrap in plastic wrap. Refrigerate for at least 30 minutes. Cut each roll into seven slices. Refrigerate any leftovers. **Yield:** about 7 dozen.

SPINACH CHEESE PUFFS
Patricia Gould, Canaan, New Hampshire

Friends and family request that I make these golden brown puffs every year on Christmas Eve. The tasty little treats are so good, you can't help but pop them in your mouth.

    1 cup milk
1/2 cup butter (no substitutes)

    1 teaspoon salt
    1 cup all-purpose flour
    4 eggs
    1 package (10 ounces) frozen chopped spinach,
      thawed and well drained
    1 cup (4 ounces) shredded Swiss cheese
1/2 cup grated Parmesan cheese

In a saucepan, bring the milk, butter and salt to a boil over medium heat. Add flour all at once and stir until a smooth ball forms. Remove from the heat; let stand for 5 minutes. Add eggs, one at a time, beating well after each addition. Continue beating until the mixture is smooth and shiny. Stir in spinach and cheeses. Line baking sheets with foil and grease the foil. Drop batter by tablespoonfuls 1-1/2 in. apart onto prepared baking sheets. Bake at 375° for 23-28 minutes or until puffed and golden brown. Remove to wire racks. Serve warm. Refrigerate any leftovers. **Yield:** about 3-1/2 dozen.

DRIED BEEF SPREAD
Margaret Sas, Ocean City, Maryland

This tasty spread is handy for entertaining during the holidays because you can make it ahead of time. For a festive presentation, chill it for an hour or two, shape it into a ball and roll in chopped nuts.

    1 package (2-1/2 ounces) sliced dried beef
    2 packages (8 ounces *each*) cream cheese, cubed
    2 tablespoons milk
    1 tablespoon chopped green onion
1/2 teaspoon dill weed
1/4 teaspoon hot pepper sauce
Crackers *or* party rye bread

Place beef in a food processor or blender; cover and process until chopped. Add the cream cheese, milk, onion, dill and hot pepper sauce; cover and process until well blended. Serve with crackers or bread. **Yield:** 2 cups.

ZIPPY CHEESE BITES
Bernita Ebel, Norfolk, Nebraska

You'll need just four ingredients to assemble this extra-rich blend. Picante sauce adds a little kick to the cheesy squares that are wonderful served warm on crackers.

    5 eggs
    3 cups (12 ounces) shredded Monterey Jack
      cheese
    3 cups (12 ounces) shredded cheddar cheese
3/4 cup picante sauce
Assorted crackers

In a bowl, beat eggs; add cheeses. Pour half into a greased 13-in. x 9-in. x 2-in. baking dish. Spoon the picante sauce over top. Top with the remaining egg mixture. Bake, uncovered, at 350° for 25-30 minutes or until a knife inserted near the center comes out clean. Let stand for 15 minutes. Cut into 1-in. squares. Serve warm on crackers. Refrigerate any leftovers. **Yield:** about 9-1/2 dozen.

CRUNCHY SWISS 'N' HAM SNACKS
Shirley Privratsky, Winterset, Iowa

These crumb-coated bites always bring many favorable comments. The recipe makes a big batch, so you're sure to have plenty for that special party.

        2 cups ground fully cooked ham
        2 cups stiff mashed potatoes*
        1 cup (4 ounces) shredded Swiss cheese
    1/3 cup mayonnaise
    1/4 cup finely chopped onion
        1 egg, beaten
        1 teaspoon prepared mustard
    1/4 teaspoon pepper
 1-1/4 cups crushed cornflakes

In a bowl, combine the first eight ingredients; mix well. Cover and refrigerate for 1 hour or until easy to handle. Shape into 1-in. balls; roll in cornflakes until coated. Place in a lightly greased 15-in. x 10-in. x 1-in. baking pan. Bake at 350° for 25-30 minutes or until golden brown. Serve warm. Refrigerate any leftovers. **Yield: about 5 dozen. *Editor's Note:** For best results, use homemade mashed potatoes prepared without milk or butter.

HOLIDAY MUSHROOM APPETIZERS
Patricia Kile, Greentown, Pennsylvania

A friend served these wedges at an open house. With English muffins as a base, they're quick and convenient to make—and sure to be a hit with mushroom lovers in your crowd!

        4 ounces fresh mushrooms, finely chopped
    1/4 cup butter *or* margarine, softened, *divided*
        1 jar (5 ounces) sharp American cheese spread
 1-1/2 teaspoons mayonnaise
    1/2 teaspoon seasoned salt
    1/2 teaspoon Italian seasoning
    1/4 teaspoon garlic salt
        6 English muffins, split

In a small skillet, saute mushrooms in 1 tablespoon butter; drain and cool. In a bowl, combine the cheese spread, mayonnaise, seasoned salt, Italian seasoning, garlic salt, mushroom mixture and remaining butter. Spread onto cut side of each muffin; cut each into eight wedges. Place on a baking sheet. Broil 4 in. from the heat for 4 minutes or until golden brown. Refrigerate any leftovers. **Yield: 4 dozen.**

CHEESY SAUSAGE DIP
Curtis Cole, Dallas, Texas

The garlic really comes through in this crowd-pleasing cheese dip. It's one of our family's all-time favorites. I serve it in a slow cooker with a basket of tortilla chips alongside.

        1 pound ground beef
        1 pound bulk pork sausage
        2 tablespoons all-purpose flour
        1 can (10-3/4 ounces) condensed cream of
          mushroom soup, undiluted
        1 can (10 ounces) diced tomatoes and
          green chilies, undrained
        1 medium onion, chopped
        1 tablespoon garlic powder
        2 pounds process American cheese, cubed
Tortilla chips

In a large saucepan, cook beef and sausage over medium heat until no longer pink; drain. Sprinkle with flour. Add the soup, tomatoes, onion and garlic powder; mix well. Bring to a boil; cook and stir for 2 minutes or until thickened. Reduce heat. Stir in the cheese until melted. Serve warm with tortilla chips. Refrigerate any leftovers. **Yield: 8 cups.**

FESTIVE FRUIT 'N' FRANKS
Edie DeSpain, Logan, Utah

A zesty mix of apricot preserves, pineapple, mandarin oranges and apple gives a sweet treatment to cocktail franks. Serve this and you'll receive compliments galore.

        1 tablespoon cornstarch
    1/3 cup lemon juice
        1 jar (10 to 12 ounces) apricot preserves
    1/2 teaspoon ground cinnamon
        1 package (12 ounces) miniature smoked
          sausage links
        1 can (8 ounces) pineapple chunks, drained
        1 can (11 ounces) mandarin oranges, drained
        1 large red apple, cut into chunks

In a saucepan, combine cornstarch and lemon juice until smooth. Add the preserves and cinnamon. Bring to a boil over medium heat; cook and stir for 2 minutes or until thickened. Add sausage and pineapple; stir to coat. Cook for 5 minutes or until heated through. Just before serving, stir in oranges and apple. Serve warm. Refrigerate any leftovers. **Yield: 10-12 servings.**

BACON-WRAPPED
WATER CHESTNUTS
Penny Patterson, Kent City, Michigan

A sweet glaze coats these crunchy appetizers that get gobbled up at parties as soon as I put them on the plate.

 1-1/2 pounds sliced bacon
        3 cans (8 ounces *each*) whole water chestnuts,
          drained and halved
 1-1/2 cups packed brown sugar
    3/4 cup ketchup
    3/4 cup mayonnaise*

Cut bacon strips into thirds. Wrap each strip around a water chestnut and secure with a toothpick. Place in an ungreased 13-in. x 9-in. x 2-in. baking dish. Bake, uncovered, at 400° for 30-35 minutes or until bacon is crisp, turning once; drain. Meanwhile, combine the remaining ingredients; pour over water chestnuts. Bake 6-8 minutes longer or until hot and bubbly. **Yield: about 8-1/2 dozen. *Editor's Note:** Light or fat-free mayonnaise may not be substituted for regular mayonnaise.

CRANBERRY CHUTNEY
June Formanek, Belle Plaine, Iowa
(Pictured below)

Its beautiful ruby hue makes this chutney ideal for the holiday season. The interesting mix of ingredients is a zesty complement to both meat and poultry.

> 1 pound fresh *or* frozen cranberries
> 2-1/2 cups sugar
> 1 cup water
> 1/2 teaspoon salt
> 1/2 teaspoon ground cinnamon
> 1/2 teaspoon ground cloves
> 1 medium onion, chopped
> 1 medium tart apple, peeled and cubed
> 1 medium pear, peeled and cubed
> 1 cup raisins
> 1/4 cup lemon juice
> 1 tablespoon grated lemon peel
> 1/2 cup chopped walnuts
> Cooked pork chops *or* roast turkey *or* chicken

In a saucepan, combine the cranberries, sugar, water, salt, cinnamon and cloves. Bring to a boil; reduce heat. Simmer, uncovered, for 10 minutes. Add the onion, apple and pear; cook for 5 minutes. Remove from the heat; stir in raisins, lemon juice and peel. Cover and refrigerate for 8 hours or overnight. Just before serving, stir in the walnuts. Serve with meat. **Yield:** about 7 cups.

ASIAN SPICED TURKEY
K. Fung, Stoneham, Massachusetts
(Pictured on pages 26 and 27)

I have my mother and our Chinese heritage to thank for this moist and savory turkey. The vanilla, aniseed and apple juice make the basting sauce unique.

> 2 to 3 celery ribs
> 1 to 2 green onions
> 1 turkey (16 to 20 pounds)
> 3 cups water, *divided*
> 1 cup soy sauce
> 1/4 cup sugar
> 1/4 cup apple juice
> 1 teaspoon vanilla extract
> 1/2 teaspoon garlic powder
> 1/2 teaspoon ground ginger
> 1/8 teaspoon aniseed, crushed
> 1/8 teaspoon *each* ground cinnamon, nutmeg
> and cloves

Place celery and onions inside the turkey cavity. In a small bowl, combine 1 cup water, soy sauce, sugar, apple juice, vanilla and seasonings; mix well. Place turkey, breast side up, on a rack in a roasting pan; pour remaining water into the pan. Pour 1/4 cup soy sauce mixture into the cavity and another 1/4 cup over turkey; set remaining sauce aside. Bake, uncovered, at 325° for 3-1/2 to 4 hours or until a meat thermometer reads 180°, basting occasionally with remaining sauce. When turkey begins to brown, cover lightly with foil. Cover and let stand for 20 minutes before carving. **Yield:** 18-20 servings.

RAISIN-STUDDED APPLE STUFFING
Teri Lindquist, Gurnee, Illinois
(Pictured on page 26)

This is the only stuffing my family will permit on our holiday table. With Italian sausage and a blend of so many great flavors, it's almost a meal in itself. No wonder it won first prize in a local recipe contest!

> 1 cup raisins
> 1-1/2 cups orange juice, *divided*
> 2 cups chopped celery
> 1 large onion, chopped
> 1 cup butter *or* margarine, *divided*
> 1 pound bulk Italian sausage
> 1 package (14 ounces) crushed herb-seasoned
> stuffing
> 4 medium tart apples, peeled and chopped
> 1 cup chopped pecans
> 2 cups chicken broth
> 2 teaspoons dried thyme
> 1/2 teaspoon pepper

In a saucepan, bring raisins and 1 cup orange juice to a boil. Remove from the heat; set aside (do not drain). In a skillet, saute celery and onion in 1/2 cup butter until tender. Transfer to a large bowl. In the same skillet, cook sausage over medium heat until no longer pink; drain. Add sausage, stuffing, apples, pecans, remaining orange juice and reserved raisins to celery mixture. In a saucepan, melt the remaining butter; add broth, thyme and pepper. Pour over stuffing mixture; mix well. Place in two greased 13-in. x 9-in. x 2-in. baking dishes. Cover and bake at 325° for 1 hour. Uncover; bake 10 minutes longer or until lightly browned. Refrigerate any leftovers. **Yield:** 18 cups.

SPICED SQUASH RINGS
Kathy Biesheuvel, Broadus, Montana
(Pictured on page 27)

If you're tired of traditional sweet potatoes, this side dish is a tasty alternative. The cornmeal gives it a pleasant texture, and there's a nice balance between sweetness and spice.

    2 medium acorn squash
    2 eggs
    1/4 cup milk
    1/2 cup cornmeal
    1/4 cup packed brown sugar
    3/4 teaspoon ground cinnamon
    1/4 teaspoon salt
    1/4 teaspoon ground nutmeg
    1/3 cup butter *or* margarine, melted

Wash squash. Cut into 1/2-in. rings; remove and discard seeds and membranes. In a shallow dish, beat eggs and milk. In another shallow dish, combine the cornmeal, brown sugar, cinnamon, salt and nutmeg; mix well. Dip squash rings into egg mixture, then into cornmeal mixture; turn to coat. Place in a greased 15-in. x 10-in. x 1-in. baking pan; drizzle with butter. Cover and bake at 400° for 25 minutes. Uncover; bake 10 minutes longer or until the squash is tender. **Yield:** 6-8 servings.

ORANGE BONBON CAKE
Ann Loveland, Dothan, Alabama
(Pictured on page 27)

The sunshiny flavor in this cake's layers, filling and frosting reminds me of the cheerful lady who gave me the recipe. I've made it for 30 years' worth of special occasions.

    1/2 cup butter *or* margarine, softened
    1-1/4 cups sugar
    1/4 cup sour cream
    1 teaspoon vanilla extract
    2 cups all-purpose flour
    2-1/2 teaspoons baking powder
    1/2 teaspoon salt
    1/4 teaspoon baking soda
    1/2 cup orange juice
    5 egg whites
    FILLING:
    3/4 cup sugar
    2 tablespoons all-purpose flour
    1/2 cup orange juice
    1/2 cup butter *or* margarine, melted
    5 egg yolks, beaten
    1/2 cup chopped pecans
    1/2 cup flaked coconut
    FROSTING:
    1/4 cup all-purpose flour
    1 cup orange juice
    1/2 cup butter *or* margarine, softened
    1/2 cup shortening
    1 cup sugar
    1 teaspoon vanilla extract
    1/2 teaspoon salt
    Candied fruit, optional

In a mixing bowl, cream butter and sugar. Beat in the sour cream and vanilla. Combine the dry ingredients; add to creamed mixture alternately with orange juice. In another mixing bowl, beat egg whites until stiff peaks form; fold into batter. Pour into two greased and floured 8-in. round cake pans. Bake at 350° for 25-30 minutes or until a toothpick comes out clean. Cool for 10 minutes before removing from pans to wire racks to cool completely. For filling, combine sugar and flour in a saucepan. Gradually stir in orange juice and butter. Bring to a boil over medium heat; cook and stir for 2 minutes or until thickened. Remove from the heat. Stir 1/2 cup of hot mixture into egg yolks; return all to the pan, stirring constantly. Cook and stir over medium-low heat until a thermometer reads 160° and mixture is thickened. Remove from the heat; stir in pecans and coconut. Cool. For frosting, combine flour and orange juice in a saucepan until smooth. Cook and stir over medium-low heat for 5 minutes or until thickened. Remove from the heat; cool. In a mixing bowl, cream the butter, shortening and sugar. Beat in vanilla and salt. Add cooled orange juice mixture; beat for 5 minutes or until fluffy. Split each cake into two layers; place one on a serving plate. Spread with a third of the filling. Repeat layers twice. Top with remaining cake layer. Frost top and sides of cake. Garnish with candied fruit if desired. **Yield:** 12-16 servings.

LIME STRAWBERRY SURPRISE
Arline Wertz, Millington, Tennessee
(Pictured on page 26)

Eye-catching in Christmas colors, this dish looks deliciously decorative on the table. Its combination of fruitiness and nutty crunch is surprisingly simple to create.

    1 package (3 ounces) lime gelatin
    1 can (8 ounces) crushed pineapple, drained
    1 package (8 ounces) cream cheese, softened
    1/2 cup mayonnaise
    1/2 cup chopped pecans
    1 package (3 ounces) cherry *or* strawberry gelatin

Prepare lime gelatin according to package directions. Refrigerate until partially set, about 1 hour. Stir in pineapple. Pour into an 8-cup bowl or mold. Cover and refrigerate until firm, about 3 hours. Beat cream cheese and mayonnaise until smooth; stir in pecans. Spread over lime gelatin. Refrigerate until firm, about 2 hours. Prepare strawberry gelatin according to package directions; cool slightly. Carefully pour over cream cheese layer. Refrigerate until firm, about 3 hours or overnight. **Yield:** 8-10 servings. **Editor's Note:** This recipe was doubled for a 4-qt. trifle bowl.

HOLIDAY FEAST. Shown clockwise from top right: Orange Bonbon Cake (p. 25), Asian Spiced Turkey (p. 24), Spiced Squash Rings (p. 25), Raisin-Studded Apple Stuffing (p. 24) and Lime Strawberry Surprise (p. 25).

ONION POTATO ROLLS
Fancheon Resler, Bluffton, Indiana

As a 4-H judge, I sampled a variation of these light, golden rolls at our county fair. With a touch of onion, it's a real blue-ribbon recipe that wins raves whenever I serve it.

2 packages (1/4 ounce *each*) active dry yeast
1/2 cup warm water (110° to 115°)
1 cup warm milk (110° to 115°)
1 cup mashed potato flakes
1/2 cup butter *or* margarine, softened
1/2 cup packed brown sugar
2 eggs
1 envelope onion soup mix
1 teaspoon salt
2 cups whole wheat flour
2-1/2 to 3 cups all-purpose flour
TOPPING:
1 egg
1/4 cup dried minced onion

In a mixing bowl, dissolve yeast in warm water. Add the next eight ingredients; mix well. Stir in enough all-purpose flour to form a soft dough. Turn onto a floured surface; knead until smooth and elastic, about 6-8 minutes. Place in a greased bowl, turning once to grease top. Cover and let rise in a warm place until doubled, about 1 hour. Punch the dough down; divide into 18 pieces. Shape each into a ball. Place 2 in. apart on greased baking sheets. Cover and let rise until doubled, about 30 minutes. Beat egg; brush over rolls. Sprinkle with dried onion. Bake at 350° for 15-18 minutes or until golden brown. Remove to wire racks to cool. **Yield:** 1-1/2 dozen.

STUFFED APPLES WITH CUSTARD SAUCE
Nancy Snyder, Albuquerque, New Mexico

Chock-full of old-fashioned goodness, this baked apple recipe is yummy…to the core. Its sauce drizzles on so smooth and creamy, it rivals the fanciest desserts.

1 cup chopped walnuts
1 cup raisins
1/2 cup sugar
1/4 cup butter *or* margarine, melted
8 medium unpeeled tart apples
1/2 cup water
CUSTARD SAUCE:
1/2 cup sugar
1 tablespoon all-purpose flour
1/8 teaspoon salt
1 cup milk
1 cup whipping cream
4 egg yolks, lightly beaten
1/4 teaspoon vanilla extract

In a blender or food processor, combine the walnuts, raisins and sugar; cover and process until ground. Stir in butter; set aside. Core apples and remove enough pulp to leave a 1-in. shell. Fill each apple with about 1/4 cup nut mixture. Place in a greased shallow 3-qt. baking dish. Pour water around apples. Bake, uncovered, at 375° for 50-60 minutes

or until tender. Meanwhile, for custard sauce, combine the sugar, flour and salt in a saucepan. Gradually stir in milk and cream until smooth. Bring to a boil over medium heat; cook and stir for 2 minutes or until thickened. Remove from the heat. Stir a small amount of hot milk mixture into egg yolks; return all to the pan, stirring constantly. Bring to a gentle boil; cook and stir for 2 minutes. Remove from the heat; stir in vanilla. Cool. Serve over warm apples. Refrigerate any leftovers. **Yield:** 8 servings.

FESTIVE FRUIT SALAD
Peggy Feist, Eatonton, Georgia

Here's a salad that won't remain on the dinnertime sidelines. Each time I serve it, it earns lots of compliments for being so colorful and refreshing.

3/4 cup sugar
1/3 cup all-purpose flour
1 cup milk
1 can (20 ounces) crushed pineapple, drained
2 tablespoons butter *or* margarine
4 medium unpeeled red apples, cut into chunks
1 cup green grapes
1 cup chopped pecans, toasted
1/4 cup red maraschino cherries, quartered
1/4 cup green maraschino cherries, quartered

In a saucepan, combine sugar and flour. Stir in milk and pineapple until blended. Bring to a boil over medium heat, stirring constantly. Cook and stir for 2 minutes or until thickened. Remove from the heat; add butter. Cool. In a bowl, combine the apples, grapes, pecans and cherries. Add dressing; stir to coat. Cover and refrigerate until serving. **Yield:** 10-12 servings.

RICH 'N' CREAMY POTATO CASSEROLE
Mary White, Pawnee City, Nebraska

My husband, a pastor, and our three children enjoy these potatoes so much that I don't wait until the holidays to make them. This casserole often comes out when we invite church members over for a family-style meal.

6 medium potatoes
2 cups (16 ounces) sour cream
2 cups (8 ounces) shredded cheddar cheese
4 tablespoons butter *or* margarine, melted, *divided*
3 green onions, thinly sliced
1 teaspoon salt
1/4 teaspoon pepper

Place potatoes in a saucepan; cover with salted water. Bring to a boil. Reduce heat; cover and simmer until tender. Drain and cool. Peel and grate potatoes; place in a bowl. Add the sour cream, cheddar cheese, 3 tablespoons butter, green onions, salt and pepper. Transfer to a greased 2-1/2-qt. baking dish. Drizzle with remaining butter. Bake, uncovered, at 350° for 30-35 minutes or until heated through. Refrigerate any leftovers. **Yield:** 8-10 servings.

CHRISTMAS BROCCOLI SALAD
Terri Puffenbarger, Blue Grass, Virginia

Horseradish gives this well-seasoned salad a special zing. The radishes and broccoli add a festive Yule flair—but I prepare it for my husband and our two boys all year long.

      3/4 cup cold water
      3 egg yolks
      3 tablespoons vinegar
      2 tablespoons sugar
      1 tablespoon cornstarch
      3/4 teaspoon salt
      2 tablespoons prepared horseradish
      4 cups broccoli florets (about 1 medium bunch)
Grated radishes

In a blender, combine the first six ingredients; cover and process until smooth. Transfer to a saucepan; cook and stir over low heat until a thermometer reads 160° and mixture is thickened. Stir in horseradish. Cover and refrigerate until chilled. Meanwhile, place broccoli in a saucepan; add 1 in. of water. Bring to a boil; reduce heat. Cover and simmer for 5-8 minutes or until crisp-tender. Rinse with cold water; drain well. Transfer to a serving bowl; cover and refrigerate. Just before serving, spoon sauce over broccoli. Garnish with radishes. **Yield:** 4 servings.

HOT TURKEY SALAD SANDWICHES
Jeanne Lester, Newport News, Virginia

Our family looks forward to these day-after-Christmas sandwiches featuring leftover turkey. When presented alongside coleslaw and cranberry sauce, they make another meal worth celebrating.

      2 to 3 cups diced cooked turkey
      2 celery ribs, diced
      1 small onion, diced
      2 hard-cooked eggs, chopped
      3/4 cup mayonnaise
      1/2 teaspoon salt
      1/4 teaspoon pepper
      6 hamburger buns, split

In a bowl, combine the turkey, celery, onion, eggs, mayonnaise, salt and pepper. Spoon into buns. Wrap each in foil. Bake at 400° for 20-25 minutes or until heated through. **Yield:** 6 servings.

CARROT SOUFFLE
Martha Sorrell, Louisville, Kentucky

This recipe is rooted in my backyard garden. It's an excellent way to dress up veggies. My six grandchildren are happy to eat their carrots when they're dished up like this.

1-1/2 cups soft bread crumbs
      1 cup milk
      3 eggs, *separated*
      2 cups finely grated carrots
      1/2 cup finely chopped celery

      3 tablespoons minced fresh parsley
      1 tablespoon grated onion
      1 teaspoon salt
      1/4 teaspoon pepper
      1/4 teaspoon cream of tartar

In a bowl, soak bread crumbs in milk. Lightly beat egg yolks; add to crumbs with carrots, celery, parsley, onion, salt and pepper. Mix well. In a mixing bowl, beat egg whites and cream of tartar until stiff peaks form. Gently fold into carrot mixture. Transfer to a greased 2-qt. baking dish. Bake, uncovered, at 325° for 40-45 minutes or until a knife inserted near the center comes out clean. **Yield:** 6-8 servings.

BAKED CHICKEN AMANDINE
Pauline Strickland, Friendship, Wisconsin

On busy winter evenings, this saucy casserole is a minute-saving mainstay. Often, I serve it with twice-baked potatoes, salad and dessert. It's fine for family, company and potlucks.

      3 to 4 cups cubed cooked chicken
      1 package (10 ounces) frozen chopped broccoli, thawed
      2 cans (10-3/4 ounces *each*) condensed cream of chicken soup, undiluted
      1 cup mayonnaise*
      2 cups (8 ounces) shredded cheddar cheese
      1 cup crushed butter-flavored crackers (about 25)
      1/4 cup butter *or* margarine, melted
      1/2 cup sliced almonds

In a greased 13-in. x 9-in. x 2-in. baking dish, layer chicken and broccoli. In a bowl, combine soup and mayonnaise; spoon over the broccoli. Sprinkle with cheese. Combine the crackers and butter; sprinkle over the cheese. Top with almonds. Bake, uncovered, at 350° for 45-50 minutes or until golden brown. **Yield:** 6-8 servings. *Editor's Note: Light or fat-free mayonnaise may not be substituted for regular mayonnaise.*

JEWELED HAM GLAZE
Marian Platt, Sequim, Washington

When it comes to creating a gorgeous holiday entree, this glaze is tops. If your kitchen time's limited, try preparing it ahead so it's on hand in the refrigerator.

      1 jar (12 ounces) currant jelly
      1/2 cup light corn syrup
      1/4 cup lemon juice
      1/2 teaspoon grated lemon peel
      1/4 teaspoon ground cloves
      1/4 teaspoon ground cinnamon
      1/4 teaspoon ground allspice
1-1/3 cups chopped mixed candied fruit

In a saucepan, combine the first seven ingredients. Bring to a boil; reduce heat. Simmer, uncovered, for 5-7 minutes. Remove from the heat. Add candied fruit and mix well. Spoon glaze over ham during the last 30 minutes of baking time. **Yield:** 2-1/2 cups.

Holiday Cookies

SOUR CREAM CUTOUTS
Bobbie Hanks, Tulsa, Oklahoma
(Pictured on page 32)

As a city kid, I was always eager to visit my grandparents on their Oklahoma farmstead. There I acquired my taste for country food, like these tender cookies with buttery icing.

   1 cup butter (no substitutes), softened
   2 cups sugar
   3 eggs
   6 cups all-purpose flour
   2 teaspoons baking soda
   1/2 teaspoon salt
   1 cup (8 ounces) sour cream
FROSTING:
   1/2 cup butter (no substitutes), softened
   4 cups confectioners' sugar
   3 tablespoons milk
Food coloring, optional

In a mixing bowl, cream butter and sugar. Add eggs, one at a time, beating well after each addition. Combine dry ingredients; add to the creamed mixture alternately with sour cream (dough will be sticky). Cover and refrigerate for 2 hours or until easy to handle. On a floured surface, roll out dough to 1/4-in. thickness. Cut into desired shapes with cookie cutters dipped in flour. Place 1 in. apart on greased baking sheets. Bake at 375° for 8-12 minutes or until lightly browned. Cool for 1-2 minutes before removing to wire racks. For frosting, in a mixing bowl, beat the butter, confectioners' sugar and milk until smooth. Add food coloring if desired. Frost cookies. **Yield:** about 9 dozen.

SWEETHEART COOKIES
Pamela Esposito, Smithville, New Jersey
(Pictured on page 32)

These rounds filled with fruit preserves were blue-ribbon winners at the county fair 2 years running. A family favorite, they never last past December 25!

   3/4 cup butter (no substitutes), softened
   1/2 cup sugar
   1 egg yolk
1-1/2 cups all-purpose flour
   2 tablespoons raspberry *or* strawberry preserves
Confectioners' sugar, optional

In a mixing bowl, cream butter and sugar. Add egg yolk; mix well. Stir in the flour by hand. On a lightly floured surface, gently knead dough for 2-3 minutes or until thoroughly combined. Roll into 1-in. balls. Place 2 in. apart on greased baking sheets. Using the end of a wooden spoon handle, make an indention in the center of each. Fill each with 1/4 teaspoon preserves. Bake at 350° for 13-15 minutes or until edges are lightly browned. Remove to wire racks. Dust warm cookies with confectioners' sugar if desired. Cool. **Yield:** about 2 dozen.

PEPPERMINT COOKIES
Mrs. Robert Nelson, Des Moines, Iowa
(Pictured on page 33)

Some 40 years ago, I whipped up these minty morsels as a way to use leftover candy canes…and my daughter has enthusiastically anticipated the cookies for Christmas ever since!

   1 cup shortening
   1/2 cup sugar
   1/2 cup packed brown sugar
   2 eggs
1-1/2 teaspoons vanilla extract
2-3/4 cups all-purpose flour
   1 teaspoon salt
   1/2 teaspoon baking soda
   1/2 cup crushed peppermint candies

In a mixing bowl, cream shortening and sugars. Add the eggs, one at time, beating well after each addition. Beat in vanilla. Combine the dry ingredients; gradually add to the creamed mixture. Stir in crushed candies. Shape into a 15-in. roll; wrap in plastic wrap. Refrigerate for 4 hours or until firm. Unwrap and cut into 1/8-in. slices. Place 2 in. apart on ungreased baking sheets. Bake at 375° for 6-8 minutes or until edges begin to brown. Remove to wire racks to cool. **Yield:** about 6 dozen.

ORANGE COOKIES
Diane Myers, Meridian, Idaho
(Pictured on page 33)

Dozens of these citrusy delights travel along with me to the school and church functions I attend during the holidays. The abundant orange flavor is refreshing.

   1 cup shortening
1-1/2 cups sugar
   1 cup buttermilk
   3 eggs
   2/3 cup orange juice
4-1/2 teaspoons grated orange peel
   3 to 3-1/2 cups all-purpose flour
   1 teaspoon baking soda
   1 teaspoon baking powder
ICING:
4-1/4 cups confectioners' sugar
   1/4 teaspoon orange extract
   1/3 to 1/2 cup orange juice

In a mixing bowl, cream shortening and sugar. Add the buttermilk, eggs, orange juice and peel. Combine the dry ingredients; gradually add to the creamed mixture. Drop by teaspoonfuls 2 in. apart onto ungreased baking sheets. Bake at 375° for 10 minutes or until lightly browned. Remove to wire racks to cool. For icing, combine the confectioners' sugar, orange extract and enough orange juice to achieve desired consistency. Spread over cooled cookies. **Yield:** about 12 dozen.

FUDGY MACAROON BARS
Beverly Zdurne, East Lansing, Michigan
(Pictured on page 32)

Sweet tooths make a beeline for my dessert tray whenever these rich squares show up. They're attractive on the platter and delectable with fudge and coconut.

    4 squares (1 ounce *each*) unsweetened chocolate
    1 cup butter (no substitutes)
    2 cups sugar
    1 cup all-purpose flour
  1/4 teaspoon salt
    1 teaspoon vanilla extract
    3 eggs, lightly beaten
FILLING:
    3 cups flaked coconut
    1 can (14 ounces) sweetened condensed milk
    1 teaspoon vanilla extract
  1/2 teaspoon almond extract
TOPPING:
    1 cup (6 ounces) semisweet chocolate chips
  1/2 cup chopped walnuts

In a saucepan over low heat, melt chocolate and butter. Remove from the heat; cool slightly. Stir in the sugar, flour, salt, vanilla and eggs; mix well. Spread half of the batter into a greased 13-in. x 9-in. x 2-in. baking pan. In a bowl, combine the filling ingredients. Spoon over chocolate layer. Carefully spread remaining chocolate mixture over filling. Bake at 350° for 35-40 minutes or until the sides pull away from the pan. Immediately sprinkle with chocolate chips. Allow chips to soften for a few minutes, then spread over bars. Sprinkle with walnuts. Cool completely before cutting. **Yield:** 3 dozen.

CREAM CHEESE MACADAMIA COOKIES
Lillie Grove, Beaver, Oklahoma

With their soft cake-like texture and subtle orange flavor, these tender drop cookies are sure to liven up holiday tea parties and luncheons. They also make great gifts for loved ones and tasty treats to have on hand throughout the season.

  1/2 cup butter (no substitutes), softened
    1 package (8 ounces) cream cheese, softened
  3/4 cup packed brown sugar
    4 teaspoons grated orange peel
    2 teaspoons vanilla extract
1-1/2 cups all-purpose flour
    2 teaspoons baking powder
  3/4 cup coarsely chopped salted macadamia nuts*
    or almonds

In a mixing bowl, cream the butter, cream cheese, brown sugar, orange peel and vanilla. Combine flour and baking powder. Gradually add to the creamed mixture; mix well. Fold in nuts. Cover and refrigerate for 1 hour or until firm. Drop by rounded teaspoonfuls 2 in. apart onto ungreased baking sheets; flatten slightly. Bake at 400° for 9-11 minutes or until lightly browned. Remove to wire racks to cool. **Yield:** about 3-1/2 dozen. ***Editor's Note:** If using unsalted macadamia nuts, add 1/4 teaspoon salt to the dough.

PINEAPPLE STAR COOKIES
Sarah Lukaszewicz, Batavia, New York
(Pictured above)

I'm grateful my neighbor gave me this special recipe. When you see the cookies' pretty shape and savor the pineapple filling and sweet frosting, you'll know they're worth the effort.

    1 cup butter (no substitutes), softened
    1 package (8 ounces) cream cheese, softened
    2 cups all-purpose flour
FILLING:
  3/4 cup sugar
4-1/2 teaspoons all-purpose flour
    1 can (8 ounces) crushed pineapple, drained
FROSTING:
    1 cup confectioners' sugar
    2 tablespoons butter (no substitutes), melted
    2 tablespoons milk
  1/2 teaspoon vanilla extract
  1/2 cup chopped walnuts

In a mixing bowl, cream the butter and cream cheese. Add flour and mix well. Cover and refrigerate for 2 hours or until easy to handle. Meanwhile, in a saucepan, combine sugar and flour; add pineapple. Cook over low heat until mixture is thickened, stirring frequently. Cover and refrigerate. Divide dough in half. On a lightly floured surface, roll out each portion to 1/8-in. thickness. Cut into 3-in. squares. Place 1 in. apart on ungreased baking sheets. To form star, make a 1-1/4-in. cut from each corner toward center (do not cut through center). Place 1/4 teaspoon of pineapple filling in the center of each. Fold every other point toward the center, overlapping pieces; press lightly to seal. Bake at 375° for 8-10 minutes or until set. Remove to wire racks to cool. For frosting, combine the confectioners' sugar, butter, milk and vanilla until smooth. Drizzle over cookies; sprinkle with walnuts. **Yield:** 5 dozen.

COLORFUL COOKIE CREATIONS. Shown clockwise from top left: Fudgy Macaroon Bars (p. 31), Orange Cookies (p. 30), Peppermint Cookies (p. 30), Sour Cream Cutouts (p. 30) and Sweetheart Cookies (p. 30).

ENVELOPES OF FUDGE
Donna Nowicki, Center City, Minnesota

Sealed inside a golden crust is a delicious special delivery—a fudgy walnut filling that's almost like a brownie. These cookies are like two treats in one.

1/2 cup butter (no substitutes), softened
1 package (3 ounces) cream cheese, softened
1-1/4 cups all-purpose flour
FILLING:
1/2 cup sugar
1/3 cup baking cocoa
1/4 cup butter (no substitutes), softened
1 egg yolk
1/2 teaspoon vanilla extract
1/8 teaspoon salt
1/2 cup finely chopped walnuts

In a mixing bowl, cream butter and cream cheese. Gradually add the flour. On a lightly floured surface, knead until smooth, about 3 minutes. Cover and refrigerate for 1-2 hours or until easy to handle. For filling, combine the sugar, cocoa, butter, yolk, vanilla and salt. Stir in walnuts; set aside. On a lightly floured surface, roll into a 12-1/2-in. square; cut into 2-1/2-in. squares. Place a rounded teaspoonful of filling in center of each square. Bring two opposite corners to center. Moisten edges with water and pinch together. Place 1 in. apart on lightly greased baking sheets. Bake at 350° for 18-22 minutes or until lightly browned. Remove to wire racks to cool. **Yield:** 25 cookies.

DATE NUT MERINGUES
Antoinette Capelli, Williston, Florida

It's always nice to make different recipes to enhance my Christmas cookie selection each year. Since I like to bake but not fuss too much, these old-fashioned chews are a good choice.

3 egg whites
1 cup sugar
1/2 teaspoon vanilla extract
1 package (8 ounces) chopped dates
1-1/2 cups chopped pecans

In a mixing bowl, beat egg whites until soft peaks form. Gradually add sugar; beat until stiff peaks form, about 6 minutes. Beat in vanilla. Fold in dates and pecans. Drop by rounded teaspoonfuls 2 in. apart onto lightly greased baking sheets. Bake at 325° for 12-15 minutes or until firm to the touch. Remove to wire racks to cool. Store in an airtight container. **Yield:** 6 dozen.

CRANBERRY OAT COOKIES
Marjorie Goertzen, Chase, Kansas

These cookies that I adapted from another recipe call to mind ones my mother used to bake. Instead of stirring in raisins like she did, though, I add bright red cranberries for festive flair.

2/3 cup butter (no substitutes), softened
2/3 cup packed brown sugar

2 eggs
1-1/2 cups all-purpose flour
1-1/2 cups old-fashioned oats
1 teaspoon baking soda
1 teaspoon ground cinnamon
1/2 teaspoon salt
1-1/4 cups dried cranberries
1 cup chopped pecans, toasted
2/3 cup vanilla *or* white chips

In a mixing bowl, cream butter and brown sugar. Add eggs; mix well. Combine the dry ingredients; gradually add to the creamed mixture. Stir in the remaining ingredients. Drop by tablespoonfuls 3 in. apart onto ungreased baking sheets. Bake at 375° for 10-12 minutes or until golden brown. Remove to wire racks to cool. **Yield:** about 4 dozen.

HOLIDAY MELTING MOMENTS
Lorraine Sheeley, Waynesboro, Pennsylvania

The name of these cookies says it all—they melt in your mouth. Adding candied cherries to the dough makes them merry.

1 cup butter (no substitutes), softened
3/4 cup packed brown sugar
1 egg
3/4 teaspoon vanilla extract
1-3/4 cups cake flour
1/2 teaspoon baking soda
1/2 teaspoon cream of tartar
1/8 teaspoon salt
1/2 cup quartered red *and/or* green candied cherries
1/2 cup chopped pecans

In a mixing bowl, cream butter and brown sugar. Beat in the egg and vanilla. Combine the dry ingredients; gradually add to the creamed mixture. Stir in cherries and pecans. Drop by teaspoonfuls 2 in. apart onto well-greased baking sheets. Bake at 350° for 8-10 minutes or until golden brown. Remove to wire racks to cool. **Yield:** 5 dozen.

PECAN-TOPPED SUGAR COOKIES
Betty Lech, St. Charles, Illinois

This recipe dresses up refrigerated cookie dough with cream cheese and coconut. Folks love the almond flavor.

1 can (8 ounces) almond paste
1 package (3 ounces) cream cheese, softened
1/4 cup flaked coconut
1 tube (18 ounces) refrigerated sugar cookie dough
1 cup pecan halves

In a mixing bowl, beat almond paste and cream cheese. Add coconut; mix well. Cut cookie dough into 1/2-in. slices; divide each slice into four portions. Roll into balls. Place 2 in. apart on greased baking sheets. Shape 1/2 teaspoonfuls of almond mixture into balls; place one on each ball of dough. Lightly press pecans into tops. Bake at 350° for 10-12 minutes or until lightly browned. Remove to wire racks to cool. **Yield:** about 3-1/2 dozen.

CHOCOLATE-DIPPED PEANUT LOGS
Patricia Grall, Hortonville, Wisconsin

A cookie exchange introduced me to these fancy peanut butter treats. They're eye-catching for the holidays and bake sales.

1 cup creamy peanut butter
1/2 cup butter *or* margarine, softened
1/2 cup shortening
1 cup sugar
1 cup packed brown sugar
2 eggs
2-1/2 cups all-purpose flour
1-1/2 teaspoons baking soda
1 teaspoon baking powder
1/4 teaspoon salt
8 ounces dark chocolate candy coating
2/3 cup ground salted peanuts

In a mixing bowl, cream the peanut butter, butter, shortening and sugars. Add eggs, one at a time, beating well after each addition. Combine the dry ingredients; gradually add to the creamed mixture. Shape into 2-in. logs. Place 2 in. apart on ungreased baking sheets. Bake at 350° for 8-10 minutes or until lightly browned. Remove to wire racks to cool. In a microwave or heavy saucepan, melt candy coating; stir until smooth. Dip one end of each cookie into coating; shake off excess. Dip into peanuts. Place on waxed paper to harden. **Yield:** about 8-1/2 dozen.

ANGEL WINGS
R. Lane, Tenafly, New Jersey

I knew I'd hit on a winner with these crispy roll-ups when my sister first sampled them. After one taste, she was so impressed she asked me to bake her wedding cake!

1 cup cold butter (no substitutes), cubed
1-1/2 cups all-purpose flour
1/2 cup sour cream
10 tablespoons sugar, *divided*
1 tablespoon ground cinnamon, *divided*

In a bowl, cut butter into flour until the mixture resembles coarse crumbs. Stir in the sour cream. Turn onto a lightly floured surface; knead 6-8 times or until mixture holds together. Shape into four balls; flatten slightly. Wrap in plastic wrap; refrigerate for 4 hours or overnight. Unwrap one ball. Sprinkle 2 tablespoons sugar on waxed paper; coat all sides of ball with sugar. Roll into a 12-in. x 5-in. rectangle between two sheets of waxed paper. Remove top sheet of waxed paper. Sprinkle dough with 3/4 teaspoon cinnamon. Lightly mark a line down the center of the dough, making two 6-in. x 5-in. rectangles (Fig. 1). Starting with a short side, roll up, jelly-roll style (Fig. 2), to the

Fig. 1   **Fig. 2**

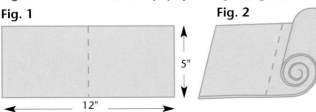

center mark; peel waxed paper away while rolling. Repeat with other short side. Wrap in plastic wrap; freeze for 30 minutes. Repeat three times. Place remaining sugar on waxed paper. Unwrap one roll. Cut into 1/2-in. slices; dip each side into sugar. Place 2 in. apart on ungreased baking sheets. Bake at 375° for 12 minutes or until golden brown. Turn cookies; bake 5-8 minutes longer. Remove to wire racks to cool. **Yield:** about 3 dozen.

CHOCOLATE-FILLED SPRITZ
Theresa Ryan, White River Junction, Vermont

I found this delicious cookie recipe years ago. Over time, I decided to liven them up with a creamy chocolate filling.

1 cup butter (no substitutes), softened
2/3 cup sugar
1 egg
1/2 teaspoon vanilla extract
1/2 teaspoon lemon *or* orange extract
2-1/4 cups all-purpose flour
1/4 teaspoon baking powder
1/4 teaspoon salt
4 squares (1 ounce *each*) semisweet chocolate

In a mixing bowl, cream butter and sugar. Beat in the egg and extracts. Combine the dry ingredients; gradually add to the creamed mixture. Using a cookie press fitted with the disk of your choice, press dough 2 in. apart onto ungreased baking sheets. Bake at 350° for 10-12 minutes or until set (do not brown). Remove to wire racks to cool. Melt the chocolate; spread over the bottom of half of the cookies; top with remaining cookies. **Yield:** about 3 dozen.

CHERRY ICEBOX COOKIES
Patty Courtney, Jonesboro, Texas

As a home economics teacher, I often supplied treats for school functions. These delectable cookies were always popular.

1 cup butter (no substitutes), softened
1 cup sugar
1/4 cup packed brown sugar
1 egg
1 teaspoon vanilla extract
3-1/4 cups all-purpose flour
1/2 teaspoon baking soda
1/2 teaspoon ground cinnamon
1/4 teaspoon cream of tartar
1/4 cup maraschino cherry juice
4-1/2 teaspoons lemon juice
1/2 cup chopped walnuts
1/2 cup chopped maraschino cherries

In a mixing bowl, cream butter and sugars. Beat in egg and vanilla. Combine dry ingredients; gradually add to creamed mixture. Add cherry and lemon juices. Stir in nuts and cherries. Shape into four 12-in. rolls; wrap each in plastic wrap. Refrigerate for 4 hours or until firm. Unwrap and cut into 1/4-in. slices. Place 2 in. apart on ungreased baking sheets. Bake at 375° for 8-10 minutes or until the edges begin to brown. Remove to wire racks to cool. **Yield:** about 6 dozen.

CREATIVE CONFECTIONS. Shown clockwise from top left: Double Chocolate Fudge (p. 37), Grandma's Butterscotch Candy (p. 37) and Christmas Eve Mice (p. 37).

Seasonal Sweets

GRANDMA'S BUTTERSCOTCH CANDY
Catherine Rothermel, Columbus, Ohio
(Pictured on page 36)

The recipe for this wonderfully buttery candy was handed down from my grandma. My brothers, sisters and I love it now as much as we did when we were little…and so do our families. It's become a cherished tradition.

    2 cups sugar
    2/3 cup water
    1/4 teaspoon cream of tartar
    2 tablespoons butter (no substitutes)
    1 teaspoon vanilla extract

Butter a 13-in. x 9-in. x 2-in. pan; set aside. In a heavy saucepan, combine the sugar, water and cream of tartar. Bring to a boil, without stirring, over medium heat until a candy thermometer reads 300° (hard-crack stage). Syrup will turn a golden color. Remove from the heat; stir in butter and vanilla. Return to heat. Cook and stir until thermometer returns to 300°. Pour into prepared pan. Cool. Break into pieces. **Yield:** about 3/4 pound. **Editor's Note:** See the box on page 39 for information about testing your candy thermometer.

CHRISTMAS EVE MICE
Margene Pons, West Valley City, Utah
(Pictured on page 36)

Assembling these merry mice is so much fun that the kids will definitely want to help. My daughter gave me the recipe, along with a warning…your guests just might think these treats are too cute to eat!

    24 double-stuffed cream-filled chocolate sandwich
       cookies
     1 cup (6 ounces) semisweet chocolate chips
     2 teaspoons shortening
    24 red maraschino cherries with stems,
       well drained
    24 milk chocolate kisses
    48 sliced almonds
     1 small tube green decorative icing gel
     1 small tube red decorative icing gel

Carefully twist cookies apart; set aside the halves with cream filling. Save plain halves for another use. In a microwave or heavy saucepan, melt chocolate chips and shortening; stir until smooth. Holding each cherry by the stem, dip in melted chocolate, then press onto the bottom of a chocolate kiss. Place on the cream filling of cookie, with cherry stem extending beyond cookie edge. For ears, place slivered almonds between the cherry and kiss. Refrigerate until set. With green gel, pipe holly leaves on the cream. With red gel, pipe holly berries between leaves and pipe eyes on each chocolate kiss. Store in an airtight container at room temperature. **Yield:** 2 dozen.

DOUBLE CHOCOLATE FUDGE
Florence Hasty, Louisiana, Missouri
(Pictured on page 36)

Anyone who's fond of chocolate will like this smooth, nutty fudge twice as much. I enjoy making several batches when Christmas rolls around. It doesn't last long at our house during December festivities!

    1 package (12 ounces) semisweet chocolate chips
    1 can (14 ounces) sweetened condensed milk,
      divided
    2 teaspoons vanilla extract, *divided*
    1 cup chopped walnuts, *divided*
    1 package (11-1/2 ounces) milk chocolate chips

Line a 9-in. square pan with foil and butter the foil; set aside. In a heavy saucepan, melt semisweet chocolate chips with 1/2 cup plus 3 tablespoons milk over low heat. Remove from the heat; stir in 1 teaspoon vanilla and 1/2 cup walnuts. Spread into prepared pan. In a saucepan, melt milk chocolate chips with remaining milk. Remove from the heat; stir in remaining vanilla and walnuts. Spread over first layer. Cover and refrigerate until firm. Remove from pan and cut into 1-in. squares. Store at room temperature. **Yield:** 6-1/2 dozen.

CHEWY WALNUT-APRICOT CANDIES
Edie Sword, Weslaco, Texas

A bit old-fashioned, these fruit-and-nut confections are both different and delicious. Munching on one is like biting into a fresh-picked gift from the orchard.

        4 cups apricot nectar *or* apple juice
    4-3/4 cups sugar, *divided*
        4 envelopes unflavored gelatin
        1 cup cold water
        3 cups finely chopped walnuts
    1-1/2 teaspoons orange extract
    Pinch salt

Line a 13-in. x 9-in. x 2-in. pan with foil and butter the foil; set aside. In a heavy saucepan, combine the apricot nectar and 4 cups of sugar. Bring to a boil over medium heat until a candy thermometer reads 238° (soft-ball stage), stirring occasionally. Remove from the heat and set aside. In a bowl, soften gelatin in water; let stand for 1 minute. Stir into apricot mixture until the gelatin is dissolved. Stir in the walnuts, orange extract and salt. Pour into the prepared pan. Cover and let stand at room temperature overnight. Place the remaining sugar in a shallow bowl. Cut the candy into 1-in. squares and roll in sugar. Place on baking sheets. Let stand for at least 1 hour. Roll candies in additional sugar if desired. Store in an airtight container at room temperature. **Yield:** about 8 dozen. **Editor's Note:** See the box on page 39 for information about testing your candy thermometer.

ORANGE CAPPUCCINO CREAMS
Lucile Cline, Wichita, Kansas

As holiday gifts, these mocha-orange morsels are sure to be a sweet success. The delighted response they get is well worth the kitchen time it takes to make them.

12 squares (1 ounce *each*) white baking chocolate, chopped
6 tablespoons whipping cream, *divided*
1-1/2 teaspoons orange juice
1/2 teaspoon orange extract
1-1/2 teaspoons finely grated orange peel
1/4 cup finely chopped walnuts
2 teaspoons instant coffee granules
4 squares (1 ounce *each*) semisweet chocolate, chopped

In a heavy saucepan over low heat, melt white chocolate with 1/4 cup cream, orange juice, extract and peel. Stir until chocolate is melted. Remove from the heat; stir in walnuts. Cool for 10-12 minutes. Using a small spoon, fill 1-in. foil or paper candy cups about two-thirds full. Chill for 30 minutes. Meanwhile, combine coffee granules and remaining cream in a saucepan. Cook and stir over low heat until coffee is dissolved. Add semisweet chocolate; cook and stir until chocolate is melted. Spoon about 1/2 teaspoon over white chocolate in each cup. Store in an airtight container at room temperature. **Yield:** about 4 dozen.

NUTTY CITRUS CANDY
Betty Hostetler, Ocean Park, Washington

A friend shared the recipe for these refreshing tangy-sweet goodies. Whenever I need a guaranteed crowd-pleaser, I roll them out by the dozens.

1 package (1 pound) confectioners' sugar
1 package (12 ounces) vanilla wafers, crushed
1 can (6 ounces) frozen orange juice concentrate, thawed
1/2 cup butter *or* margarine, melted
1-1/2 to 2 cups ground walnuts

In a bowl, combine the confectioners' sugar, wafer crumbs, orange juice and butter; mix well. Shape into 3/4-in. balls, then roll in walnuts. Cover and refrigerate for at least 24 hours before serving. Store in an airtight container in the refrigerator. **Yield:** 8 dozen.

COCONUT BONBONS
Beverly Cray, Epping, New Hampshire

My family and friends never fail to include these chocolates on their Christmas wish list. Luckily, this recipe makes a big batch—so my supply meets the candy demand.

1/2 cup butter (no substitutes), softened
2 pounds confectioners' sugar
1 can (14 ounces) sweetened condensed milk
4 cups chopped pecans
1 package (10 ounces) flaked coconut

1 teaspoon vanilla extract
2 cups (12 ounces) semisweet chocolate chips
1 tablespoon shortening

In a mixing bowl, cream butter and sugar. Add the milk, pecans, coconut and vanilla; mix well. Shape into 1-in. balls. Refrigerate for 30-45 minutes or until firm. In a microwave or heavy saucepan, melt the chips and shortening; stir until smooth. Dip balls and place on waxed paper to harden. Store in an airtight container at room temperature. **Yield:** about 21 dozen. **Editor's Note:** Candies can be frozen for up to 3 months before dipping in chocolate. Thaw in refrigerator before dipping.

TUTTI-FRUTTI
Florence Munger, Malone, New York

Red and green cherries make these treats look festive. Substitute any fruit in the amount that pleases your palate.

3 tablespoons butter (no substitutes), melted
1/4 cup evaporated milk
1 teaspoon almond extract
1/4 teaspoon salt
4-1/4 to 4-3/4 cups confectioners' sugar
1/4 cup *each* chopped citron, candied pineapple, and green and red candied cherries
3/4 cup finely chopped almonds

In a large bowl, combine the butter, milk, almond extract and salt. Gradually stir in confectioners' sugar until a stiff dough is formed. Turn onto a surface lightly dusted with confectioners' sugar. Knead 15-20 times or until mixture forms a smooth ball. Knead in candied fruit. Shape into 1-in. balls, then roll in almonds. Cover and refrigerate for 1 hour. Store in an airtight container in the refrigerator. **Yield:** about 3 dozen.

ALMOND PEANUT BUTTER SQUARES
Thelma Waggoner, Hopkinsville, Kentucky

I don't need to shop around to find a Christmas gift that's always appreciated. These easy-to-prepare squares suit anyone who has a taste for homemade treats.

1 cup sugar
1/2 cup honey
1/2 cup light corn syrup
1 cup creamy peanut butter
1 teaspoon vanilla extract
2-1/2 cups whole unblanched almonds

Line a 9-in. square pan with foil and butter the foil; set aside. Butter the sides of a heavy saucepan; add the sugar, honey and corn syrup. Bring to a boil over medium heat, stirring constantly. Boil, without stirring, for 2 minutes. Remove from the heat; immediately stir in the peanut butter, vanilla and almonds. Pour into prepared pan. Let stand at room temperature until completely cool. Cut into squares. Individually wrap pieces in foil or waxed paper; twist ends. **Yield:** about 6 dozen.

CINNAMON WALNUTS
Betty Rogers, Walnut Creek, California

Sampling just one of these taste-bud tempters almost always leads to another. That's why I package a big batch in gift tins for happy holiday snackers.

        1 cup sugar
    1/3 cup evaporated milk
        1 teaspoon ground cinnamon
    1/4 teaspoon salt
    1/4 teaspoon vanilla extract
        3 cups walnut halves

In a heavy saucepan, combine the sugar, milk, cinnamon and salt. Cook over medium heat, without stirring, until a candy thermometer reads 238° (soft-ball stage). Remove from the heat; stir in vanilla and walnuts. Spread onto waxed paper to harden. Break into pieces. Store in an airtight container at room temperature. **Yield:** about 1 pound. **Editor's Note:** See the box below right for information on testing your candy thermometer.

COCONUT APRICOT BALLS
Geraldine Seney, Grand Rapids, Michigan

These zesty confections are filled with fresh fruity flavor. They make a nice addition to any candy tray.

        2 cups dried apricots
        1 cup flaked coconut
        1 tablespoon grated lemon peel
        1 tablespoon grated orange peel
    1/4 cup sugar, *divided*
        1 to 2 teaspoons orange juice, optional

In a food processor, combine the apricots, coconut, lemon peel and orange peel. Cover and process for 1-2 minutes or until blended. Sprinkle work surface with 1 tablespoon of sugar. Knead apricot mixture until smooth, about 15-20 times. Add orange juice if necessary to moisten mixture. Shape into 1-in. balls and roll in remaining sugar. Store in an airtight container. **Yield:** about 4 dozen.

PECAN DIVINITY
Carolyn Weber, Vicksburg, Mississippi

The table at our Sunday school Christmas party has a spot reserved for my divinity. I love making candy and have recruited my husband to help…between nibbles.

        2 cups sugar
        1 cup water
        1 jar (7 ounces) marshmallow creme
        1 teaspoon vanilla extract
    1-1/2 cups chopped pecans

In a large heavy saucepan, combine the sugar and water. Cook over medium heat, without stirring, until a candy thermometer reads 250° (hard-ball stage). Remove from the heat; stir in marshmallow creme, vanilla and pecans. Continue stirring until candy cools and begins to hold its

shape when dropped from a spoon. Quickly drop by heaping teaspoonfuls onto waxed paper-lined baking sheets. Store in an airtight container at room temperature. **Yield:** 4 dozen. **Editor's Note:** See the box below for information about testing your candy thermometer.

DATE PECAN FUDGE
F. Lovejoy, Winfield, West Virginia

As a new bride, my Texas-born mother made this recipe to remind her of home. Now, when I make the mellow date-filled candy, happy family times come to mind.

    3/4 cup butter (no substitutes)
        3 cups sugar
    2/3 cup evaporated milk
    1/2 cup chopped dates
        12 ounces white candy coating, coarsely chopped
        4 cups miniature marshmallows
        1 cup chopped pecans
        1 teaspoon vanilla extract

In a large heavy saucepan, combine the butter, sugar and milk. Cook and stir over low heat until sugar is dissolved. Bring to a boil; boil and stir for 4 minutes. Add dates; boil and stir for 1 minute. Remove from the heat; stir in candy coating and marshmallows until melted. Beat until smooth. Add pecans and vanilla; beat with a wooden spoon until glossy. Pour into a buttered 13-in. x 9-in. x 2-in. pan. Let stand at room temperature overnight. Cut into squares. **Yield:** 3 pounds.

MICROWAVE WALNUT BRITTLE
Thelma Brown, Fulton, Illinois

Looking for a snappy standout? This brittle is simple to make in the microwave. Plus, it'll bring on the compliments quickly.

        2 cups chopped walnuts *or* black walnuts
        1 cup sugar
    1/2 cup light corn syrup
    1/2 teaspoon salt
        1 tablespoon butter (no substitutes)
        1 teaspoon vanilla extract
        1 teaspoon baking soda

In a covered 1-1/2-qt. microwave-safe glass dish, microwave the walnuts, sugar, corn syrup and salt on high for 4 minutes. Stir; cook 4 minutes longer. Stir in butter and vanilla. Cover and microwave on high for 2 minutes. Add baking soda; stir quickly until light and foamy. Immediately pour onto a lightly buttered baking sheet; spread until very thin. When cool, break into small pieces. Store in an airtight container at room temperature. **Yield:** 1-1/4 pounds. **Editor's Note:** This recipe was tested in a 700-watt microwave.

> ● It is recommended that you test your candy thermometer before each use by placing it in a pot of boiling water; the thermometer should read 212°. Adjust your recipe temperature up or down based on your test.

Festive Desserts

CANDY ORANGE SLICE FRUITCAKE
Anna Minegar, Zolfo Springs, Florida
(Pictured on page 41)

My version of Yule fruitcake has a citrusy twist. When you share it, be prepared to pass around the recipe.

>   1 cup butter *or* margarine, softened
>   2 cups sugar
>   2 cups applesauce
>   4 eggs
>   1/2 cup buttermilk
>   1 pound candy orange slices
>   2 cups chopped pecans
>   2 cups flaked coconut
> 1-1/2 cups candied cherries
>   1 package (8 ounces) chopped dates
> 3-1/2 cups all-purpose flour, *divided*
>   1 teaspoon baking soda
>   1/8 teaspoon salt

In a mixing bowl, cream the butter and sugar. Beat in the applesauce, eggs and buttermilk. In a bowl, combine the orange slices, pecans, coconut, cherries, dates and 1 cup of flour; toss to coat. Combine the baking soda, salt and remaining flour; add to the buttermilk mixture. Fold in orange slice mixture. Pour into a greased and floured 10-in. tube pan. Bake at 300° for 1-3/4 to 2 hours or until a toothpick inserted near the center comes out clean. Cool for 10 minutes before removing from pan to a wire rack to cool completely. **Yield:** 10-12 servings.

WHITE CHOCOLATE CREAM PIE
Yalonda Rennie, Bakersfield, California
(Pictured on page 41)

This dessert earned a prize at our church picnic. It's a favorite with my husband—he can't get enough of white chocolate.

>   2/3 cup sugar
>   1/3 cup cornstarch
>   3 cups milk
>   3 egg yolks, beaten
>   4 squares (1 ounce *each*) white baking chocolate
>   1 teaspoon vanilla extract
>   1 pastry shell (9 inches), baked
> **HOLLY GARNISH:**
>   4 squares (1 ounce *each*) white baking chocolate,
>   *divided*
> Red and green paste food coloring
> **TOPPING:**
>   2 cups whipping cream
>   3 tablespoons confectioners' sugar

In a saucepan, combine sugar and cornstarch; gradually whisk in milk until smooth. Cook and stir over medium heat until mixture comes to a boil. Cook and stir for 2 minutes. Remove from the heat. Stir a small amount of hot mixture into egg yolks; return all to saucepan, stirring constantly.

Bring to a gentle boil; cook and stir for 2 minutes. Remove from the heat; stir in white chocolate and vanilla. Let stand until chocolate is melted, stirring occasionally. Pour into pastry shell. Refrigerate for at least 3 hours. For holly leaf garnish, melt 1/2 ounce white chocolate; tint with red food coloring. Place in a pastry or plastic bag. Pipe 24 small berries on waxed paper; let stand until hardened. Melt remaining white chocolate; tint with green food coloring. Spread into a rectangle on waxed paper; let stand at room temperature until hardened. Using a 1-1/2-in. holly leaf cookie cutter, cut 18 leaf shapes. Just before serving, beat cream and confectioners' sugar until soft peaks form; spread over pie. Garnish with holly leaves and berries. Store in the refrigerator. **Yield:** 8 servings. **Editor's Note:** For a simple garnish, use spearmint leaves and red-hot candies.

CHOCOLATE CHERRY CHEESECAKE
Kathy Speer, La Crosse, Wisconsin
(Pictured on page 41)

My love for chocolate-covered cherries inspired this fun and fancy cheesecake that's perfect for Christmas.

>   2 cups chocolate wafer crumbs (about 32 wafers)
>   6 tablespoons butter (no substitutes), melted
> **CHEESECAKE:**
>   4 packages (8 ounces *each*) cream cheese,
>   softened
>   1 cup sugar
>   2 teaspoons vanilla extract
>   4 eggs
>   4 squares (1 ounce *each*) white baking chocolate,
>   melted and cooled
>   1 jar (10 ounces) maraschino cherries, drained,
>   rinsed and quartered
>   1/2 cup chopped pecans
> **TOPPING:**
>   3 squares (1 ounce *each*) semisweet chocolate
>   2 tablespoons butter (no substitutes)
> 1-1/2 teaspoons shortening, *divided*
>   1/2 square (1/2 ounce) white baking chocolate

In a bowl, combine chocolate crumbs and butter. Press onto the bottom and 1 in. up the sides of a greased 10-in. springform pan. Bake at 350° for 8 minutes. Cool on a wire rack. In a mixing bowl, beat the cream cheese until smooth. Add sugar and vanilla; mix well. Add eggs; beat on low speed just until combined. Stir in melted chocolate; mix well. Gently fold in cherries and pecans. Pour into crust. Bake at 350° for 50-55 minutes or until center is almost set. Cool on a wire rack for 10 minutes. Carefully run a knife around edge of pan to loosen; cool 1 hour longer. Refrigerate overnight. Remove side of pan. In a saucepan, melt semisweet chocolate, butter and 1 teaspoon shortening until smooth. Cool for 2 minutes; pour over cheesecake. Spread over the top and let it run down the sides. Cool. In a small saucepan, melt white chocolate and remaining shortening. Drizzle over the top. Cool. Store in the refrigerator. **Yield:** 12 servings.

DAZZLING DESSERTS. Shown clockwise from top left: Chocolate Cherry Cheesecake (p. 40), White Chocolate Cream Pie (p. 40) and Candy Orange Slice Fruitcake (p. 40).

CINNAMON CHOCOLATE ANGEL PIE

Donna Torres, Grand Rapids, Minnesota

Our Christmas dinner wouldn't be complete without a festive finale. I've served this satisfying pie for so many years that it's become a holiday tradition.

   2 egg whites
   1/2 teaspoon white vinegar
   1/2 cup sugar
   1/8 to 1/4 teaspoon ground cinnamon
   1 pastry shell (9 inches), baked
FILLING:
   2 egg yolks
   1/4 cup water
   1 cup (6 ounces) semisweet chocolate chips
   1 cup whipping cream
   1/4 cup sugar
   1/4 teaspoon ground cinnamon

In a mixing bowl, beat egg whites and vinegar on medium speed until foamy. Combine sugar and cinnamon; gradually beat into egg whites, 1 tablespoon at a time, on high until stiff peaks form. Spread into the pastry shell. Bake at 325° for 20-25 minutes or until meringue is lightly browned. Cool. For filling, whisk egg yolks and water in a saucepan. Add chocolate chips; cook and stir over low heat until a thermometer reads 160° and mixture is thickened (do not boil). Cool. Spread 3 tablespoons over meringue; set remainder aside. In a mixing bowl, beat the cream, sugar and cinnamon until stiff peaks form. Spread half over the chocolate layer. Fold reserved chocolate mixture into remaining whipped cream; spread over top. Chill for 6 hours or overnight. Refrigerate any leftovers. **Yield:** 8-10 servings.

HARVEST PIE

Roberta Murren, Overbrook, Kansas

There's a cornucopia of fall flavor baked into this eye-pleasing pie. Even my husband, who isn't a cranberry fan, loves it. By using frozen berries, I can make it year-round.

   2 cans (8 ounces *each*) crushed pineapple
   1 package (12 ounces) fresh *or* frozen cranberries, chopped
   1 cup packed brown sugar
   1/2 cup sugar
   3 tablespoons all-purpose flour
   2 tablespoons butter *or* margarine
   3/4 cup chopped walnuts *or* pecans
   1/2 teaspoon almond extract, optional
   1/4 teaspoon salt
Pastry for double-crust pie (9 inches)

Drain pineapple, reserving 1/4 cup juice. Set pineapple aside. In a saucepan, combine the cranberries, sugars and pineapple juice. Bring to a boil; cook and stir for 5 minutes. Combine flour and pineapple; add to cranberry mixture. Cook and stir over medium heat until mixture comes to a boil; cook and stir for 2 minutes or until thickened. Remove from the heat; stir in the butter, nuts, almond extract if desired and salt. Cool. Line a 9-in. pie plate with bottom pastry; trim to 1 in. beyond edge of pie plate. Add filling.

Roll out remaining pastry to fit top of pie; place over filling. Trim, seal and flute edges. Cut slits in top. Bake at 400° for 40-45 minutes or until golden brown. Cool on a wire rack. **Yield:** 6-8 servings.

MINT CHIP CHEESE BALLS

Robin Dooley, Fort Leavenworth, Kansas

A friend brought these cheese balls as a hostess gift to our Christmas open house. They instantly caught the fancy of my family. It's like having an appetizer for dessert.

   4 packages (8 ounces *each*) cream cheese, softened
   2 cups finely chopped pecans
   1 package (11-1/2 ounces) milk chocolate chips, finely chopped
   36 starlight mints, crushed
Red and green sprinkles, optional
Chocolate wafers

In a mixing bowl, beat cream cheese until smooth; add the pecans, chocolate chips and crushed mints. Divide into four portions. Cover and refrigerate for 1 hour or until firm. Shape each portion into a ball; roll in red and green sprinkles if desired. Serve with chocolate wafers. Store in the refrigerator. **Yield:** 4 cheese balls (1-1/4 cups each).

FESTIVE CRANBERRY DESSERT SQUARES

Bev Batty, Minneapolis, Minnesota

From Thanksgiving through Christmas, you'll find these tart and tasty treats at our house. Although the recipe uses a convenient mix, it's made-from-scratch scrumptious!

   1 cup fresh *or* frozen cranberries
   2 tablespoons sugar
   2/3 cup butter *or* margarine, melted
   1 package (15.6 ounces) cranberry quick bread mix
   1 cup quick-cooking oats
   2 tablespoons brown sugar
   1 cup butterscotch caramel fudge ice cream topping*
   1/3 cup all-purpose flour
   1-1/2 cups chopped dates
   1 cup chopped walnuts

In a small bowl, combine cranberries and sugar; set aside. In a large bowl, combine the butter, quick bread mix, oats and brown sugar; set aside 1 cup for topping. Press remaining crumb mixture into a greased 13-in. x 9-in. x 2-in. baking dish. Bake at 350° for 10 minutes. Meanwhile, combine ice cream topping and flour; set aside. Sprinkle the cranberry mixture, dates and nuts over crust; drizzle with ice cream topping. Sprinkle with reserved crumb mixture. Bake for 25-30 minutes or until golden brown and bubbly. Cool in pan on a wire rack. Serve warm or cold. Store in the refrigerator. **Yield:** 15-18 servings. ***Editor's Note:** This recipe was tested with Mrs. Richardson's Butterscotch Caramel Fudge Topping.

SPECTACULAR ICE CREAM PIE
Gladys McCollum Abee, McKee, Kentucky

Biting into this melt-in-your-mouth treat is like having coffee and dessert together. To avoid the holiday baking crunch, you can make it ahead of time and store it in the freezer until you are ready to serve.

> 1 cup graham cracker crumbs (about 16 squares)
> 1/2 cup finely chopped walnuts
> 1/3 cup butter *or* margarine, melted
> 1 pint coffee ice cream *or* flavor of your choice, softened
> 1 pint vanilla ice cream, softened
> SAUCE:
> 3 tablespoons butter *or* margarine
> 1 cup packed brown sugar
> 1/2 cup half-and-half cream
> 1 cup finely chopped walnuts
> 1 teaspoon vanilla extract

In a bowl, combine the cracker crumbs, walnuts and butter; press onto the bottom and up the sides of a greased 9-in. pie plate. Bake at 375° for 8-10 minutes. Cool completely. Spread coffee ice cream over crust. Freeze for 2 hours or until firm. Repeat with vanilla ice cream. Remove pie from the freezer 15 minutes before serving. For sauce, combine butter and brown sugar in a saucepan; cook and stir over low heat for 5-6 minutes. Remove from the heat; slowly stir in cream. Cook and stir 1 minute longer. Remove from the heat; stir in walnuts and vanilla. Serve warm over slices of pie. **Yield:** 8-10 servings.

BUTTERSCOTCH BROWNIE PINWHEELS
Virginia Nicky, Bloomingdale, Illinois

A neighbor gave the recipe for these rich chewy treats to my mother when I was still in grade school, and I've been preparing them each Christmas for over 30 years. The pinwheel effect makes them extra special to share.

> 1 cup semisweet chocolate chips
> 4 tablespoons butter (no substitutes), *divided*
> 1 can (14 ounces) sweetened condensed milk
> 1 cup all-purpose flour
> 1 teaspoon vanilla extract
> Confectioners' sugar
> 1 cup butterscotch chips
> 1/2 cup chopped walnuts

Grease a 15-in. x 10-in. x 1-in. baking pan; line with waxed paper and spray the paper with nonstick cooking spray. Set aside. In a microwave or heavy saucepan, melt the chocolate chips and 2 tablespoons of butter; stir until smooth. Stir in milk, flour and vanilla; mix well. Spread into prepared pan. Bake at 325° for 8 minutes or until a toothpick inserted near the center comes out clean. Cool in pan on a wire rack for 5 minutes. Turn onto a kitchen towel dusted with confectioners' sugar. Gently peel off waxed paper. Roll up brownie in the towel, jelly-roll style, starting with a long side. Cool completely on a wire rack. Melt butterscotch chips and remaining butter. Unroll brownie; spread filling to within 1/2 in. of edges. Sprinkle with walnuts. Reroll;

wrap in foil. Refrigerate for 2 hours or until firm. Unwrap and dust with confectioners' sugar. With a sharp thin knife, cut into 1/4-in. slices. **Yield:** 5 dozen. **Editor's Note:** If brownie cracks while rolling, press together with fingers and continue rolling.

MAPLE CREAM FLUFF
Brooke Pike, Pierre, South Dakota

Mmm-maple is the featured flavor in this rich and nutty dessert. It's a nice change-of-pace contribution to a holiday potluck. I've yet to come home with leftovers!

> 2 envelopes unflavored gelatin
> 1/2 cup cold water
> 1 cup maple syrup
> 2 cups milk
> 1 cup whipping cream
> 1 cup chopped pecans, toasted, *divided*
> 2 cups vanilla wafer crumbs (about 32 wafers), *divided*

In a large saucepan, soften gelatin in cold water; let stand for 1 minute. Cook and stir over low heat (do not boil) until gelatin is dissolved, about 4 minutes. Remove from the heat; slowly stir in syrup. Set pan in ice water; whisk in milk. Continue whisking until mixture has thickened, about 10 minutes; remove pan from ice bath and set aside. In a mixing bowl, beat cream until stiff peaks form. Fold in 3/4 cup pecans and the maple mixture. Sprinkle 1 cup wafer crumbs into a 13-in. x 9-in. x 2-in. dish; top with maple mixture. Sprinkle with remaining pecans and wafer crumbs. Cover and chill for at least 6 hours or overnight. Refrigerate any leftovers. **Yield:** 12-15 servings.

CREAMY CITRUS MOUSSE
Phy Bresse, Lumberton, North Carolina

Light and fluffy, this marvelous mousse is the perfect ending to a filling holiday meal. Guests always have room for its delicate combination of tang and sweetness.

> 2 tablespoons lime juice
> 2 tablespoons sugar
> 1 package (3 ounces) lime gelatin
> 1 cup boiling water
> 1/3 cup cold water
> 2 cups whipped topping
> 1/2 cup sweetened condensed milk
> 1 tablespoon grated lime peel, optional
> 2 teaspoons orange extract
> Maraschino cherries, optional
> Additional grated lime peel, optional

Dip the rims of six individual dessert dishes in lime juice, then in sugar; set aside. In a bowl, dissolve gelatin in boiling water. Stir in cold water. Refrigerate until slightly thickened, about 30 minutes. Meanwhile, combine the whipped topping, milk, lime peel if desired and orange extract. Fold into gelatin. Spoon into dessert dishes. Refrigerate for 1 hour or until firm. Just before serving, garnish with cherries and lime peel if desired. **Yield:** 6 servings.

GIFT-WRAPPED GOODIES. Shown clockwise from top left: Cowboy Cookie Mix (p. 45), Apricot Pineapple Braid (p. 45) and Strawberry Orange Spread (p. 45).

Gifts from the Kitchen

STRAWBERRY ORANGE SPREAD
Rita MacTough, New London, Connecticut
(Pictured on page 44)

I wrap up this refreshing spread with jar toppers made from Christmasy fabric. It looks so festive tucked in a basket alongside homemade cookies.

       2 packages (10 ounces *each*) frozen sweetened
          sliced strawberries, thawed
   1/2 cup orange juice
       1 tablespoon grated orange peel
       1 package (1-3/4 ounces) powdered fruit pectin
3-1/2 cups sugar

In a kettle, combine the strawberries, orange juice and orange peel. Stir in pectin. Bring to a rolling boil over high heat, stirring constantly. Add sugar; return to a rolling boil. Boil and stir for 1 minute. Remove from the heat; skim off foam. Pour into jars or freezer containers; cool to room temperature, about 1 hour. Cover and let stand overnight or until set, but not longer than 24 hours. Refrigerate or freeze. **Yield:** about 4-1/2 cups.

APRICOT PINEAPPLE BRAID
Loranell Nelson, Goodland, Kansas
(Pictured on page 44)

Our family can't wait for Christmas morning, knowing this fruit-filled favorite will be on the table. I make several extras for our friends' breakfasts, too.

4-1/2 to 5 cups all-purpose flour
   1/2 cup sugar
       2 packages (1/4 ounce *each*) active dry yeast
1-1/2 teaspoons salt
   1/2 cup water
   1/2 cup milk
   1/4 cup butter *or* margarine
       2 eggs, beaten
FILLING:
       2 cups chopped dried apricots
       1 can (8 ounces) crushed pineapple, undrained
       1 cup packed brown sugar
   3/4 cup water
   1/4 cup orange juice
GLAZE:
       1 cup confectioners' sugar
   1/4 teaspoon vanilla extract
       1 to 2 tablespoons milk
Red and green candied cherries, optional

In a mixing bowl, combine 2 cups flour, sugar, yeast and salt. In a saucepan, heat the water, milk and butter to 120°-130°. Add to dry ingredients; beat until moistened. Beat in eggs until smooth. Stir in enough remaining flour to form a stiff dough. Turn onto a floured surface; knead until smooth and elastic, about 6-8 minutes. Place in a greased bowl, turning once to grease top. Cover and let rise in a warm place until doubled, about 1 hour. Meanwhile, combine the filling ingredients in a saucepan. Bring to a boil. Reduce heat; simmer, uncovered, for 10-15 minutes or until thickened. Cool. Punch dough down. Turn onto a lightly floured surface; divide in half. Roll each into a 16-in. x 8-in. rectangle. Place on greased baking sheets. Spoon the filling down the center third of each rectangle. On each long side, cut 1-in.-wide strips 2-1/2 in. into center. Starting at one end, fold alternating strips at an angle across filling. Pinch ends to seal and tuck under. Cover and let rise until doubled, about 30 minutes. Bake at 350° for 25-30 minutes or until golden brown. Remove from pans to wire racks to cool. For glaze, combine confectioners' sugar, vanilla and enough milk to achieve desired consistency. Drizzle over braids. Garnish with cherries if desired. **Yield:** 2 loaves.

COWBOY COOKIE MIX
Rosemary Griffith, Tulsa, Oklahoma
(Pictured on page 44)

Since half the fun of cookies is baking them, I give this merry-making mix as a gift. The ingredients look so pretty in a jar …and the cookies smell terrific coming out of the oven!

1-1/3 cups quick-cooking oats
1-1/3 cups all-purpose flour
       1 teaspoon baking powder
       1 teaspoon baking soda
   1/4 teaspoon salt
   1/2 cup chopped pecans
       1 cup (6 ounces) semisweet chocolate chips
   1/2 cup packed brown sugar
   1/2 cup sugar
ADDITIONAL INGREDIENTS:
   1/2 cup butter *or* margarine, melted
       1 egg, lightly beaten
       1 teaspoon vanilla extract

Pour oats into a wide-mouth 1-qt. glass container with a tight-fitting lid. Combine the flour, baking powder, baking soda and salt; place on top of oats. Layer with pecans, chocolate chips, brown sugar and sugar, packing each layer tightly (do not mix). Cover and store in a cool dry place for up to 6 months. **To prepare cookies:** Pour cookie mix into a large mixing bowl; stir to combine ingredients. Beat in butter, egg and vanilla. Cover and refrigerate for 30 minutes. Roll into 1-in. balls. Place 2 in. apart on greased baking sheets. Bake at 350° for 11-13 minutes or until set. Remove to wire racks to cool. **Yield:** about 3-1/2 dozen.

● Decorative jars and bottles, which many products are sold in today, can come in handy in the kitchen after they're emptied. One great use for quart-size and narrow-neck bottles with screw tops is to store dry ingredients like sugar, cornmeal or salt. Wash the bottle and dry completely before filling. If the contents become lumpy, simply shake the bottle.

PASTEL ALMOND BARK
Audrey Attoe, Lodi, Wisconsin

Cooks of all ages will find this pretty confection is a snap to prepare. It never fails to take center stage on the goody plates I make for friends.

        1 package (24 ounces) white candy coating,
            cut into 1/2-inch pieces
        2 cups pastel miniature marshmallows
        2 cups Fruit Loops
        1 cup chopped pecans
        1 cup flaked coconut

In a microwave or heavy saucepan, melt candy coating; stir until smooth. Stir in marshmallows, cereal, pecans and coconut. Drop by tablespoonfuls onto waxed paper-lined baking sheets. Cool. Store in an airtight container at room temperature. **Yield:** about 5 dozen.

FRUITY HORSERADISH SAUCE
Ellen Brainard, Holly Hill, Florida

Friends and family will get a "kick" out of this zippy condiment. It's sensational spooned over a hearty country ham, pork or beef roast.

        1 jar (12 ounces) apple jelly
        1 jar (12 ounces) pineapple preserves
        1 jar (5 ounces) prepared horseradish
        1/2 teaspoon ground mustard
Pinch pepper

In a blender or food processor, combine all ingredients. Cover and process for 1 minute or until smooth. Pour into small containers with tight-fitting lids. Store in the refrigerator for up to 3 months. **Yield:** 2-1/2 cups.

TWO-TIERED FUDGE
Christine Richburg, Brewton, Alabama

It's one good thing on top of another with this lusciously layered fudge. After your guests take a single taste, it won't be long until the compliments begin.

2-1/4 cups sugar
        1 cup milk
        3 squares (1 ounce *each*) unsweetened
            chocolate
        1 tablespoon light corn syrup
        2 tablespoons butter (no substitutes)
        1 teaspoon vanilla extract
        1/2 cup chopped nuts
SECOND LAYER:
2-1/2 cups sugar
        1/2 cup half-and-half cream
        1/2 cup milk
        1 tablespoon light corn syrup
        1/4 teaspoon salt
        2 tablespoons butter (no substitutes)
        1 teaspoon vanilla extract
        1/3 cup chopped candied cherries

Butter the sides of a heavy 2-qt. saucepan. In a saucepan, combine the first four ingredients. Cook and stir over medium heat until sugar is dissolved. Bring to a boil, stirring constantly, until mixture reaches 236° (soft-ball stage). Remove from the heat. Add butter and vanilla (do not stir). Cool to 110° without stirring. Beat vigorously by hand until fudge becomes thick and begins to lose its gloss, about 10 minutes. Immediately spread into a greased 9-in. square baking pan; set aside. For second layer, combine sugar, cream, milk, corn syrup and salt in a buttered 2-qt. saucepan. Cook and stir over medium heat until sugar is dissolved. Bring to a boil, stirring constantly until mixture reaches 236° (soft-ball stage). Remove from the heat. Add butter and vanilla (do not stir). Cool to 110° without stirring. Beat vigorously by hand until fudge begins to thicken; add cherries. Continue beating until fudge becomes thick and begins to lose its gloss, about 10 minutes. Immediately spread over first layer. Score into squares while still warm. Refrigerate until firm. Cut. Store in an airtight container at room temperature. **Yield:** about 2-1/2 pounds. **Editor's Note:** It is recommended to test your candy thermometer before each use by bringing water to a boil; the thermometer should read 212°. Adjust your recipe temperature up or down based on your test.

CINNAMON CRUNCH TRIANGLES
Liz Corley, Eufaula, Oklahoma

Adding a little sugar and spice to Yuletide is as easy as this recipe. For delivery, wrap the treats in red and green cellophane and stack in a tin or a trimmed-up gift bag.

        12 whole cinnamon graham crackers
            (5 inches x 2-1/2 inches)
        2 cups finely chopped walnuts
        1 cup butter *or* margarine
        1 cup packed brown sugar
        1/2 teaspoon ground cinnamon

Arrange graham crackers in a greased 15-in. x 10-in. x 1-in. baking pan; sprinkle with walnuts. In a saucepan, combine the butter, brown sugar and cinnamon. Cook and stir over medium heat until mixture comes to a boil. Continue cooking, without stirring, for 3 minutes. Slowly pour over crackers. Bake at 400° for 8-9 minutes or until edges are browned. Cool completely. Cut into 2-in. squares, then cut each square in half to form triangles. Store in an airtight container. **Yield:** about 5 dozen.

RASPBERRY FUDGE BALLS
Maria Jaloszynski, Appleton, Wisconsin

Here's an idea for a last-minute gift that everyone will think you fussed over. Tasters relish the delectable hint of raspberry and the creamy texture of these fudgy balls.

        1 cup (6 ounces) semisweet chocolate chips
        1 package (8 ounces) cream cheese, softened
        3/4 cup finely crushed vanilla wafers
            (about 20 cookies)
        1/4 cup seedless raspberry jam
        3/4 cup finely chopped almonds

In a microwave or heavy saucepan, melt chocolate chips; stir until smooth. Cool slightly. In a mixing bowl, beat the cream cheese and melted chocolate until smooth. Stir in the wafer crumbs and jam. Refrigerate for 4 hours or until firm. Shape into 1-in. balls; roll in almonds. Store in an airtight container in the refrigerator. **Yield:** about 2-1/2 dozen.

CHOCOLATE-CHERRY BROWNIE CUPS
Carol Walker, Spicer, Minnesota

It's so tempting to snitch one of these yummy cups, you'll want to double your recipe. That way, you'll have some to munch on right away while you package the others to give as gifts to friends and family.

> 1 cup butter (no substitutes)
> 4 squares (1 ounce *each*) semisweet chocolate
> 4 eggs
> 1-1/2 cups sugar
> 1 teaspoon vanilla extract
> 1 cup all-purpose flour
> 1-1/2 cups chopped walnuts
> 3/4 cup chopped maraschino cherries

In a microwave or double boiler, melt butter and chocolate; cool for 10 minutes. In a mixing bowl, beat eggs and sugar. Add vanilla and the chocolate mixture. Stir in flour, walnuts and cherries. Fill paper-lined muffin cups three-fourths full. Bake at 350° for 20-25 minutes or until a toothpick comes out clean. Cool for 5 minutes before removing from pans to wire racks. **Yield:** 1-1/2 dozen.

FRUITCAKE BARS
Naomi Murry, Dalton, Georgia

There's a sweet surprise in every bite of this fruitcake-like treat. The bars keep well in the freezer, so they can be enjoyed long after the holiday season's over.

> 1 cup golden raisins
> 1 cup chopped dates
> 1 cup chopped mixed candied fruit
> 1/4 cup apple juice
> 4 eggs
> 1 cup sugar
> 1 teaspoon vanilla extract
> 1 teaspoon grated orange peel
> 3/4 cup all-purpose flour
> 1/2 teaspoon salt
> 1-1/2 cups chopped walnuts

In a bowl, combine the first four ingredients; set aside. In a mixing bowl, beat eggs. Add the sugar, vanilla and orange peel; mix well. Combine flour and salt; add to sugar mixture. Stir in walnuts and the reserved fruit mixture. Spread into a greased 15-in. x 10-in. x 1-in. baking pan. Bake at 350° for 30-35 minutes or until a toothpick comes out clean. Cool in pan on a wire rack. Cut into bars. **Yield:** 4 dozen. **Editor's Note:** Baked bars may be frozen in an airtight container for up to 3 months.

BURNT PEANUTS
Sue Gronholz, Columbus, Wisconsin

As far as my family's concerned, I can't make this nutty snack too often. In fact, I save pint jars throughout the year as containers for this popular Christmas present.

> 1 cup sugar
> 1/2 cup water
> 1 teaspoon red food coloring, optional
> 2 cups raw Spanish peanuts with skins
> (no substitutes)

In a heavy saucepan, combine the sugar, water and food coloring if desired. Bring to a boil over medium heat; stir in peanuts. Cook, stirring occasionally, for 12 minutes or until peanuts are coated and no syrup remains. Spread peanuts into an ungreased 15-in. x 10-in. x 1-in. baking pan; separate with a fork. Bake at 300° for 30 minutes, stirring every 10 minutes. Cool. Store in an airtight container at room temperature. **Yield:** about 4 cups.

PEPPERMINT POPCORN
Shirley Mars, Kent, Ohio

Crisp and minty, this simple snack is a hit with all 10 of our children. For variety, try substituting other flavors of candy instead of peppermint.

> 1 pound white candy coating
> 24 cups popped popcorn
> 1/2 to 3/4 cup finely crushed peppermint candy
> (4 to 6 candy canes)

In a microwave or heavy saucepan, melt candy coating; stir until smooth. In a large bowl, combine the popcorn and crushed candy. Pour candy coating over top; toss to coat. Pour onto a waxed paper-lined baking sheet. When hardened, break apart. Store in an airtight container. **Yield:** 24 servings.

PEPPER SALAD DRESSING
Sue Braunschweig, Delafield, Wisconsin

Friends tell me they can't wait to dip into this zesty dressing. I present it, tied with a plaid ribbon, in recycled glass condiment bottles that I label with my name, the recipe's title and storage instructions.

> 1 quart mayonnaise *or* salad dressing
> 2 cups half-and-half cream
> 3 tablespoons coarsely ground pepper
> 2 tablespoons finely chopped green onions
> 1-1/2 teaspoons salt
> 3/4 teaspoon white pepper
> 3/4 teaspoon Worcestershire sauce
> 1/2 teaspoon hot pepper sauce

In a large mixing bowl, combine mayonnaise and cream; beat until smooth. Stir in remaining ingredients. Pour into salad dressing bottles or pint jars. Cover and store in the refrigerator for up to 1 week. **Yield:** 6 cups.

Christmas Tree Treat Branches Out Sweetly

SCRUMPTIOUS and lovely to look at, this pleasing pine won't last long when you set it out at your next festive gathering. The sweet stack of cream-filled puffs garnished with luscious frosting and colorful candied cherries is simply too good for guests to resist!

"I've been cooking up a Cream Puff Christmas Tree regularly for almost 50 years now, and it always receives the same enthusiastic reaction from friends and family," shares Sandra Gifford of Bridgeton, New Jersey.

What's more, the recipe Sandra uncovered in the 1950s on an advertisement for flour is a breeze to complete. "It goes together quite quickly and calls for common ingredients most cooks have on hand," she reveals.

"The little puffs are absolutely delicious. But what's really rewarding are the 'oohs' and 'aahs' I hear whenever I set it out," Sandra chuckles.

Why not raise a tasty fir for your own holiday celebration? Just follow the easy instructions here...then get set to take a "bough" as folks feast on the yummy results!

CREAM PUFF CHRISTMAS TREE

1-1/4 cups water
  2/3 cup butter (no substitutes)
1-1/4 cups all-purpose flour
  1/4 teaspoon salt
    5 eggs
FILLING:
2-1/2 cups whipping cream
  1/3 cup confectioners' sugar
  1/4 to 1/2 teaspoon rum extract, optional
ICING:
   3 cups confectioners' sugar
  1/4 to 1/3 cup half-and-half cream
Green liquid *or* **paste food coloring, optional**
Red candied cherries, optional
Additional confectioners' sugar, optional
Round pastry tip #7
  2 pastry *or* plastic bags
Serving platter *or* **covered board (10 inches)**

In a saucepan over medium heat, bring water and butter to a boil. Add flour and salt all at once; stir until a smooth ball forms. Remove from the heat; let stand for 5 minutes. Add the eggs, one at a time, beating well after each addition. Continue beating until mixture is smooth and shiny.

Drop by rounded teaspoonfuls 2 in. apart (see photo 1) onto greased baking sheets. (You will need about 62 puffs to make the tree.) Use a moistened finger to smooth any peaks.

Bake at 400° for 30-35 minutes or until golden brown. Transfer to wire racks to cool.

For filling, beat cream in a mixing bowl until soft peaks form. Gradually beat in sugar and rum extract if desired until almost stiff.

Insert round tip #7 into a pastry or plastic bag; fill with the whipped cream. With a sharp knife, cut a small slit in the side of each puff. Insert pastry tip into slit; fill each puff with whipped cream (see photo 2). Refrigerate for up to 2 hours.

For icing, combine confectioners' sugar and enough cream to achieve desired consistency. Stir in food coloring if desired.

To assemble tree: Separate puffs according to size and shape, choosing the flattest ones for the bottom layer and the smallest ones for the top. Spread the bottom of 18 puffs with icing. Place on the serving platter, forming a 9-in.-diameter solid circle.

For the second layer, spread icing on the bottoms of 18 puffs, then position above the spaces of the base layer of puffs (see photo 3).

Continue building tree in this manner (see photo 4), using about 14 puffs in third layer, about seven puffs in fourth layer, about four puffs in fifth layer and one puff on top.

To decorate: Insert round tip #7 into a pastry or plastic bag and fill with remaining icing. Drizzle over tree (see photo 5). Trim with cherries.

The completed tree may be loosely covered with plastic wrap and refrigerated for up to 2 hours. Just before serving, dust with confectioners' sugar if desired. **Yield:** 30 servings.

Shape It Up!

Here are some pointers for creating a perfectly proportioned tree...

• The fir featured here is 8-1/2 in. high x 8-3/4 in. wide with six tiers total. Use these measurements as a guide when building your tree.

• The cream puffs our kitchen staff made ranged from 1-1/2 in. to 1-3/4 in. in diameter. For uniform puffs, try using a measuring spoon to scoop up even portions of batter.

• Run out of cream puffs? Try substituting regular-size marshmallows in the center of the tree for bulk.

• Use any kind of serving platter with a slight rim to help hold the first layer of cream puffs in place.

• The sky's the limit when it comes to tree-trimming. You can dot on multicolored M&M's or decorator candies for merry ornaments...add flakes of fluffy white coconut to emulate a snowy scene...sprinkle on chopped nuts for extra crunch...use birthday candles for a bright look...or whatever comes to mind!

Photo 3. Spread icing on bottoms of the puffs and position a second layer above the spaces in the base layer.

Photo 1. Drop rounded teaspoonfuls of batter 2 in. apart onto greased baking sheets. Bake puffs as directed until golden brown.

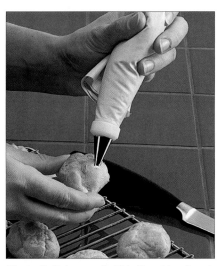

Photo 2. Cut a small slit in the side of each puff with a sharp knife. Insert the pastry tip into the slit and fill with whipped cream.

Photo 4. Spread icing on the bottoms of the puffs and position a fourth layer above the spaces in the third layer.

Photo 5. Using pastry bag and tip, drizzle remaining icing over the completed tree.

Her Chocolate-Loving Clan Is So Sweet on the Season!

DURING Christmas, Pat Adams prefers to take her sweet time—creating delicious memories by the batches.

"From October through December, we stir up homemade confections daily," Pat relates from her candy kitchen/retail shop in the small town of Dexter, Iowa. "At holiday time alone, we go through nearly *4 tons* of chocolate."

Indeed, her business, Drew's Chocolates, turns out a luscious lineup of fudge, caramels, nut clusters and countless creams with everything from banana to peanut butter at the center. "Our 'secret' ingredient," Pat adds with a smile, "is a healthy pinch of nostalgia.

"Our founder, Helen Drew, used family recipes and a fork to dip her first chocolates 73 years ago. Today, we preserve many of her time-tested techniques in making our specialty sweets.

"It does take longer to fork-dip each piece, but the thick rich coating is worth it," Pat affirms. "Plus, by making our chocolates in small batches, candy can be a family affair."

While preparing for their seasonal sugar rush, Pat and grown sons James and Jason put in 15-hour days concentrating on candy. Along with the mainstays, their holiday stock features pumpkin truffles, colorful suckers, trimmed-up nougats and Drew Drops (pecans covered in caramel and chocolate).

"To add old-fashioned flavor, we cook on an antique stove, using big copper kettles and wooden paddles," Pat reports. "Our caramel cutter, mixer and candy dippers date back to the 1920s. And we don't fudge on ingredients, like chocolate, butter and Iowa cream."

At Christmas and year-round, folks can savor the sweet fruits of Pat's labor in her two retail stores in Dexter and nearby Urbandale.

And thanks to mail order, candy fans across the nation and all the way to Japan can satisfy their craving.

"It's rewarding when people come in with their children and tell us how they visited this shop as kids," Pat shares. "Just as their parents did, they hold their little ones up to the counter to help choose the chocolates."

Editor's Note: *Drew's Chocolates is located at 426 State St., Dexter IA 50070 and at 7611 Douglas Ave., Urbandale IA 50322. To order by telephone, call 1-800/243-7397.* ☆

CHRISTMAS CONFECTION is all in the family at Drew's Chocolates where owner Pat Adams (above) and her son James (below) add dashes of sweet nostalgia to each batch.

Grandma's 'Brag' Page

CHRISTMAS CHERUB Samantha was certainly heaven-sent, according to proud Grandma Naomi Tarr of Salisbury, Maryland. The spirited sprite's costume was made by Mom Tina. Samantha looked so divine, confides Naomi, a snapshot of her adorned the family Christmas cards.

FROSTY SMALL FRY Meghan poses in front of snowy Santa sign her mom and dad made. Beams doting Grandmother Carole Hintz of Devils Lake, North Dakota, "She's my 'snowgirl'!"

ALL WRAPPED UP. Packaged in appropriate Christmas "bunting" is baby Andrea Anne Apodaca. Grandma Dorothy Meyer of Baypoint, California says Andrea is a gift that keeps on giving. "It was such a surprise to see her pop up from this gaily decorated package!" she relates.

SANTA'S SIDEKICK. Granddaughter Kalley Rose is happy to cozy up to stuffed St. Nick, pens Eunice Abel of New Richmond, Wisconsin.

SWEET DREAMS. Little Jeremy Chase (at left) "meditates" on the meaning of Christmas in this dashing dream-filled photo Grandmother Pat Vautier of Port Angeles, Washington shares.

IN TUNE with season are Betty Allison's notable grand-nieces (right). "They're just precious," she trills from Kimball, Michigan about cute quintet. Shown from left are Sarah, Hannah, twins Regina and Leah and little Lydia.

Country Decorating...

She Keeps Christmas All Over Her Country Place

By Ruth Harmon of Maysville, Kentucky

ALTHOUGH every day is special in my Maysville, Kentucky home, my family and I truly cherish Christmastime. During the holidays, I pull out all the stops, filling every room with cheery trimmings of the season!

Typically, I make sure my decorating is well under way in early November, so it's all wrapped up when our family gathers for Thanksgiving.

It's a tradition that my two children, four grandkids and five great-grandchildren plus spouses celebrate the holidays together. That's why I want the house to be Christmas-card perfect.

A welcoming feeling greets friends and family in the foyer, courtesy of a 5-foot-tall old-world Santa and a family of carolers. They're among 2 dozen animated characters that come to life around the house. The hallway's also seasoned with forest-green tiling and plants all atwinkle with lights.

Turn right into the parlor, and you'll see more shades of the holidays. Brisk touches of scarlet, ruby and cranberry spice up the soothing white interior. Red accents run from velvet curtain bows to rugs, pillows and glass pieces and create a dramatic backdrop for my crimson sofa and love seat.

The same color scheme takes a "bough" in the corner as well, decking one of eight Christmas trees I trim. Whimsical elves scale a ladder to get a closer look at my ornaments and the festive arrangements I set on lamp stands and tables.

Taste-tempting aromas waft in from the dining room across the hall—calling us together for dinner.

The table showcases an embroidered cloth with a Christmas tree pattern that's dished up in matching napkins and china. I can't think of a prettier garnish for our turkey and ham dinner with all our favorite fixings.

Between bites, the youngsters feast their eyes on the poinsettia-perked centerpieces I use to cheer up the table and buffet. Meantime, it's a treat for me to see the childrens' shining faces in the wall mirror I top off with a length of verdant evergreen roping.

By design, more greenery outlines the dining room doorway and continues

THE HIGHLIGHT of year for Ruth Harmon (above) is the holidays. She wraps home up in oodles of Christmas cheer—inside and out!

to spruce up the adjoining family room.

There, I've draped mauve and gold bows and garland along the stairway, around the tree and atop the mantel to complement my year-round motif. The cozy glow of the fireplace helps warm the decor and makes this room ideal for entertaining.

The holiday spirit comes full circle in a winsome wreath above the mantel and in Santa figures and lacy angels guarding the hearth. Our family Bible lies there opened to the story of the first Noel. It helps us keep in mind the blessed reason for the season.

Since the kitchen opens up into the family room, I can join in the merrymaking while I'm cooking.

Of course, the kitchen *does* have a holiday flavor of its own. A porcelain Nativity has a place of honor on my country-blue countertops. And the central island is covered with the fruits of my Yule baking—cutout cookies, cakes and candies, included.

Directly over the kitchen, my bal-

EVERY CORNER at Ruth's is adorned in Yuletide splendor. Beribboned evergreen in parlor (right) sports elfish trims, while tasteful tableware, swags and centerpiece flavor the dining room (below).

A CHORUS of Christmas accents is in tune with season as carolers greet guests in the foyer (above). In family room (left), glowing Noel notions brighten hearth. Rising to occasion is a garland winding up nearby stairs.

cony is particularly noteworthy at this time of year. Peeking through the banister is a quartet of choristers who serenade visitors in the family room below. In harmony with the rest of the house, my upstairs bedrooms are jolly well brimming with Christmas collectibles and knickknacks.

Since this special season is meant to be shared, I go all out in my "exterior decorating", too. Strings of white lights illuminate my crab apple trees, bushes and front entrance. Friends take a shine to my glittering grapevine tree and the gleaming reindeer wreath I round up on the door.

For a finishing touch, I string lights, greens and ribbons around my back deck and kindle electric candles in the windows. Whole families enjoy driving around our little Ohio River town on December evenings. I want every inch of my house to say, "Season's greetings".

It's the presence of my family that I value above gifts…still, the kids insist on "filling in" under my tree. It's easy to see how well they know me…many packages contain new decorations!

It's plain to see there's no place I'd rather be than home for the holidays. I hope you've enjoyed your visit. ☆

I'll Never Forget...

When Christmas Past Was Perfect!

By Susan Caltrider of Pulaski, Pennsylvania

THE CHRISTMAS when I was 10, I awoke to a world of dazzling white. I climbed out of bed and peered out the window at a great blanket of snow that covered the ground and canopied the rooftops. The pine trees were so weighted down that their wide limbs pointed to the ground. It had snowed all night.

We lived on a country dirt road where traffic could barely be heard from the distant highway, and there was not a person in sight on that glorious morning. (Back then, snowfall was measured in feet instead of inches…and, on occasion, the neighbors' horses were the only sure means of transportation.)

My two brothers and I had hardly slept a wink, or so it seemed. In our excitement, we raced down the stairs, scarcely noticing the chill in the house, the result of the furnace going out during the early morning hours.

My heart was pounding fiercely in my chest in anticipation of what Santa had brought this year. Times were tough, and although we always had plenty of food on the table and clothing to wear, expensive and multiple gifts were things we dared not ask for. But this Christmas, as we ran into the living room, I couldn't believe my eyes.

Trio of Wheels

Standing in front of the tree, all in a row, were three shiny new bicycles. I can still remember the reflection of the twinkling tree lights dancing on those brilliantly painted bikes. I later learned that my father had scrapped an old truck for parts and sold them for extra cash so he could afford those "luxury gifts".

Always, one of the nicest things about Christmas was going to Grandma's house. My brothers and I got all dressed up in our Sunday best and waited patiently for Dad to shovel so we could be on our way.

Grandma lived on the east end of town. Her home was 10 miles from ours, and Dad had to drive slowly because of the slippery roads. Wedged in the back seat between my brothers, I won-dered if the journey would ever end.

When we finally arrived and after all the relatives had been kissed "hello", we children went off to play games. The rich aroma of roasting turkey wafted through the cozy house as Grandma put the finishing touches on dinner.

Later, as I gazed across the dining table, everything looked so tempting—golden-brown turkey and stuffing, mashed potatoes with rich gravy, yams, cranberries, assorted jello salads in bright colors, and for dessert, pumpkin pie with fluffy whipped cream. Every morsel was mouth-watering!

Holiday Harmonies

After dinner, we gathered in the living room and sang Christmas carols as my uncle accompanied us on the harmonica. Smiles of joy, peace and contentment showed on every face.

While we were singing, I watched Grandma's radiant smile and thought how happy and proud she must be to have her whole family together for the first Christmas in years.

Her tree was decorated with silver tinsel and old-fashioned bubble lights, each shining a different color. Beneath it were beautifully wrapped presents. As Grandma passed out the gifts one by one, there were hugs and kisses, and happy "thank-you's" echoed in the air.

Later that evening as we were leaving town, I stared out the car window at all the houses so beautifully decorated with sparkling lights and tried to pick out the loveliest one…

So much has changed since then! Our country dirt road is paved now and lined with houses. And people are in such a hurry these days. You can still see a horse-drawn buggy, but only if you take a ride to nearby Amish country.

It's been said nothing ever stays the same…and that change is good. That may be true…but that long-ago Christmas that seemed perfect in every way is still my best memory ever!

Country Crafter's Santas Picture Christmas Past

EACH YEAR at Christmas, Diane Spoehr gets on board for the holidays by brushing up wooden St. Nicks in fine Victorian style!

"A hundred years ago, folks decorated their homes with fragrant beribboned wreaths, elaborate lace angels and beaded ornaments," details Diane. "They also set out wooden-board paintings of Santa Claus and other Yuletide themes."

Not content to let bygones be bygones, the rural Sun Prairie, Wisconsin wife and mother reproduces Victorian Santa boards in her at-home studio to adorn today's houses. "My customers use the boards just like in olden days—to enhance a staircase, hearth, corner or porch," she notes.

"Most folks have never even *heard* of my kind of crafts," Diane chuckles. "In their day, they were called dummy boards. 'Dummy' meant 'silent'. I call mine 'art' boards—but other than that, they're in the true spirit of the originals."

By the time Diane began producing the pictorials, she'd already been paint-ing wood for nearly a decade.

"A friend asked me to try a Victorian figure for her collectibles shop 8 years ago," she happily recounts. "From then on, I was hooked!"

Following in the footsteps of 19th-century artisans, Diane fashions one-of-a-kind Kris Kringles—ranging in height from 6 inches to 6 feet tall—as well as merry elves, dignified Father Christ-mases and beautiful angels.

"I create designs such as snowmen and Easter bunnies for other times of the year, too," she reports. "My husband, Sid, helps by cutting the plywood into shapes…and I use acrylic paint to apply facial features and other details.

"Our teenage sons, Zachary and Bret, do simple painting and help me haul my crafts to shows."

With all the support Diane gets from her family, she's only too happy to trim their own country abode with her brushwork at Christmastime.

"Besides that," she grins, "it's fun to see our guests do a double take when

DELIVERING a dash from the past, Diane Spoehr (above) merrily paints Victorian Santa decorations to color holidays in nostalgia.

they first notice one of my life-size carolers by the door or cats by the fire and for a moment think that they're real!"

Editor's Note: *For more information on Diane's Victorian Art Boards or to order, contact Diane Spoehr Originals, P.O. Box 361, Sun Prairie WI 53590; 1-608/837-5536.* ☆

Artist's Holiday Handiwork Sprouts from 'Gourd Pole'!

TO FIND OUT how Santa's shaping up, just stop in at Melynda Lotven's. The Columbia, Missouri crafter's busy coaxing the old elf out of his shell—with gourdgeous results!

"We call our house the 'Gourd Pole' because I style so many St. Nicks from gourds," the handy mother smiles.

Kris Kringles crop up in all sorts of forms, from short and squat to tall and skinny. Then there are the snowmen and penguins, plus Yuletide fairies.

"The shape of a gourd often determines what it will become," Melynda elaborates. "I've turned larger ones into stately elves decked out with mohair beards. Little slender gourds, on the other hand, make great angels."

Gourds from her own garden, as well as those grown by local farmers, yield an inspiring supply for Melynda. "It does take patience, though," she nods. "A gourd consists mostly of water, so each needs up to a year to dry. After that, I scrub them clean, then get creative!"

Once a design unwinds in her mind, Melynda picks up her paintbrush and gets to work. She uses acrylic colors, as well as pastels and stains, then adds fabric, yarn and little trinkets to further embellish her projects.

Melynda first cultivated her knack for gourd crafting about 10 years ago, when she and her family moved onto their forested 5-acre spread. "The previous owner left some gourds on the porch, but I was too busy unpacking to pay much attention to them," she recalls.

"By the time they caught my eye, the rinds were all moldy. Still, I saw plenty of potential!"

Since then, Melynda's become a regular exhibitor at harvest festivals, as well as an avid educator.

"I love to spread the word about gourd crafting," Melynda smiles. "My husband, Tony, and our children, Samson, Jeremiah and Olivia, also offer ideas and make their own gourd art.

"I see so many festive possibilities waiting to emerge when I pick up a gourd," Melynda continues. "But what's most heartwarming is hearing how folks use my Noel designs to brighten their homes year after year."

Editor's Note: *For more information on Melynda's gourd crafts or to visit her "Gourd Pole", write to her at Just Gourds, 5401 O'Neal Rd., Columbia MO 65202. Or visit her Web site—www.justgourds.com.*

VINE Christmas designs crop up regularly at Melynda Lotven's acres! The crafty lady fields festive figures, scenes galore by painting gourds.

Craft Section...

Merry Mats Are Neatly Rooted!

THIS coaster set sprouting engaging evergreen accents will protect your tabletop from spills, even as it brightens the entire room for Christmas.

Teri Bloom of Uniontown, Pennsylvania used durable plastic canvas to construct them. "The mats last for years," she confirms.

Materials Needed (for four coasters and holder):
Charts on this page
10-1/2-inch x 13-1/2-inch sheets of 7-count plastic canvas—two sheets of clear and one sheet of red
Worsted-weight yarn—12 yards each of green and red and 22 yards of white
Size 16 tapestry needle
Craft scissors

Finished Size: Each coaster is 4 inches square. Holder is 4-1/4 inches wide x 4-1/4 inches high x 2-1/4 inches deep.

Directions:
CUTTING: Remembering to count the bars and not the holes, cut four pieces of clear plastic canvas 26 bars x 26 bars for top of coasters. Cut four of the same-size pieces of red plastic canvas for backing of coasters.

Cut two pieces of clear plastic canvas 28 bars x 28 bars for front and back of holder and two pieces of clear plastic canvas 15 bars x 28 bars for sides. Also cut one piece of clear plastic canvas 15 bars x 28 bars for unstitched bottom of holder.

Fig. 1

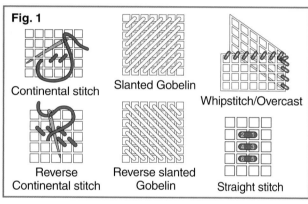

Continental stitch   Slanted Gobelin

Whipstitch/Overcast

Reverse Continental stitch   Reverse slanted Gobelin   Straight stitch

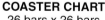

COLOR KEY
CONTINENTAL AND REVERSE CONTINENTAL STITCH
- Green
- Red
- White
SLANTED GOBELIN AND REVERSE SLANTED GOBELIN
- White
STRAIGHT STITCH
- Red
WHIPSTITCH/OVERCAST
- Red

COASTER CHART
26 bars x 26 bars

HOLDER SIDES CHART
15 bars x 28 bars

HOLDER FRONT AND BACK CHART
28 bars x 28 bars

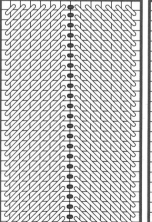
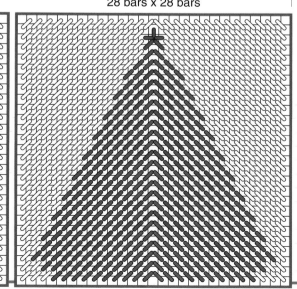

STITCHING: Working with 18-in. to 20-in. lengths of yarn, follow charts on previous page and instructions that follow to stitch the pieces. See Fig. 1 for stitch illustrations.

Do not knot yarn on back of work. Instead, leave a 1-in. tail on the back of the plastic canvas and work the next few stitches over it. To end a strand, run yarn on back of canvas under completed stitches of the same color and clip yarn close to work.

Coaster (make four): Using Conti-nental and reverse Continental stitch-es, stitch red trim on tree as shown on coaster chart. Then stitch tree shape green and background white, leaving outside edges unstitched.

Place unstitched piece of red plastic canvas backing centered on back of completed coaster and whipstitch edges together with red.

Holder: Using Continental and re-verse Continental stitches, stitch red trim on tree following holder front and back chart. Then stitch tree shape green and background white, leaving outside edges unstitched.

Using slanted Gobelin and reverse slanted Gobelin stitches, fill sides in with white as shown on holder sides chart. Using straight stitch and red, stitch ver-tical line on each side piece.

Using red, whipstitch long edges of side pieces to matching side edges of front and back of holder with right sides facing the outside. Whipstitch bottom to matching bottom edges of front, back and sides. Overcast top edge with red. ☆

Stockings Lend A Holiday Hand

KEEP pace with the season by adding these utensil holders to your holiday spread. The stockings keep tableware and napkins at hand, whether you're serving a sit-down meal or hosting a buffet, assures Margery Richmond of Lacombe, Alberta.

Materials Needed (for each):
Patterns on this page
Pencil
1/4 yard of fusible interfacing
100% cotton or cotton-blend fabrics—6-inch x 12-inch piece of green print and 3-inch x 7-inch piece of red print
2/3 yard of green double-fold bias tape
Matching all-purpose thread
Standard sewing supplies

Finished Size: Each utensil holder is 4-1/4 inches wide x 5-1/4 inches tall.

Directions:
Trace patterns onto fusible interfacing as directed. Cut out shapes on traced lines. Open cuff.

Following manufacturer's directions, fuse shapes onto wrong side of fabrics as directed on patterns. Cut out each, following outline of interfacing.

Sew bias tape to the curved edge of cuff, en-casing raw edge. Trim the ends even with the edges of the cuff.

Place two stocking pieces right sides togeth-er with edges matching. Sew pieces together with 1/4-in. seam, stitching from the top front edge of the stocking to the "X" marked on pattern. Press seam open.

Place cuff right side up on right side of stock-ing with the top edges matching. Sew the bias tape to the top edge, en-casing the raw edges of both the stocking and the cuff.

Fold stocking and attached cuff with right sides together and raw edges matching. Sew raw edges together with a 1/4-in. seam, stitching from top back of stocking around to stitching at top of foot. Turn stocking right side out. Press.

Set on your holiday table! ☆

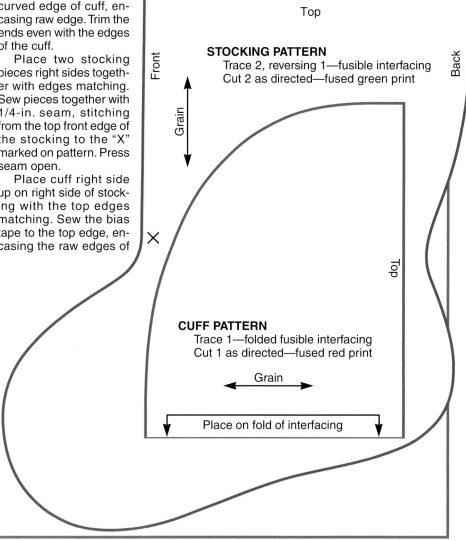

Top

STOCKING PATTERN
Trace 2, reversing 1—fusible interfacing
Cut 2 as directed—fused green print

Front

Back

Grain

CUFF PATTERN
Trace 1—folded fusible interfacing
Cut 1 as directed—fused red print

Grain

Place on fold of interfacing

Top

X

Garland Puts Happy Face on the Holidays

WHETHER you wrap these jolly old elves around the Christmas tree or drape them in a doorway or a window, they're sure to enliven any space with plenty of seasonal spirit.

Crafted by Jean Weed to deck the halls of her Sussex, Wisconsin home, the garland can be quickly assembled.

"The Santa heads are formed from Styrofoam balls," she describes. "For the rest, I used odds and ends I already had on hand."

Materials Needed:

Nine 1-1/2-inch Styrofoam balls
Serrated knife
1/4 yard of 44-inch-wide 100% cotton unbleached muslin
Compass
Red and off-white all-purpose thread
Eighteen 3/8-inch-diameter rounded wooden furniture plugs
White (tacky) glue
Acrylic craft paints—black, ivory and red
Small flat paintbrush
Paper towels
Acrylic varnish
1/3 yard of red T-shirt ribbing
White No. 8 cotton crochet thread
White acrylic curly doll hair
White angel hair or straight acrylic doll hair
Six 9mm gold jingle bells
Pom-poms—six each of 12mm white and 7mm green
Green six-strand embroidery floss
34 purchased 1/2-inch wooden cubes
Drill with 1/8-inch bit
6 yards of 1/8-inch-wide wire-edge gold metallic ribbon
2-1/4 yards of 1/8-inch-wide white satin ribbon
159 faceted 6mm green beads
Standard sewing supplies

Finished Size: Garland is about 76 inches long x 3-3/4 inches high.

Directions:

SANTA HEADS: Use knife to cut each Styrofoam ball in half for heads.

Use compass to draw eighteen 3-in.-diameter circles onto muslin. Cut out each circle. With scissors, snip a small "X" into center of each circle.

Thread hand-sewing needle with off-white thread. Hand-sew around fabric circle 1/4 in. from edge. Do not fasten off. Place circle of fabric over one half Styrofoam ball with cut "X" centered over rounded side. Pull the thread tightly to

draw up gathers to the flat side of the ball. Fasten off the thread.

Repeat, using remaining fabric circles and half-balls to make 18 heads.

Dip flat side of furniture plug into glue. Push flat side of plug into curved side of head at cut "X" for nose. Let dry. Repeat procedure, using the remaining plugs and heads.

Paint entire head and nose ivory. Let dry.

Dip handle of paintbrush into black and dab eyes onto each head above nose. Let dry.

Dip paintbrush into red and wipe excess paint onto paper towel until no brush strokes show. With an up-and-down motion, stipple noses and cheek areas on heads. Let dry.

Apply a coat of varnish to each head. Let dry.

For each of six heads, cut several 4-in.-long pieces of crochet thread. Fold each strand in half and glue fold below nose and cheek areas for beard. Trim beard so it extends about 1-1/2 in. below bottom of head.

Glue longer pieces of crochet thread around sides and top of face for hair. Cut and glue several pieces horizontally below nose for mustache. Trim hair and mustache as desired.

Repeat with remaining Santa heads, using curly doll hair for six and straight doll hair for the remaining six instead of crochet cotton.

HATS: From red ribbing, cut eighteen 3-in. x 5-in. rectangles with the ribs running parallel to the 5-in. edge.

Fold each piece of ribbing in half with short edges matching. Fold each in half again to make a 1-1/2-in. x 2-1/2-in. rectangle. Pin each to secure.

Sew hats with 1/4-in. seams as directed in instructions that follow.

Jingle bell hats (make six): Sew long and short raw edges of six folded ribbing pieces together through all layers, leaving folded edges unstitched.

Turn each hat right side out. Hand-sew a jingle bell to top of each hat opposite long back seam.

Place a hat onto each Santa with curly hair, placing seam at back of head. Place hats on heads, covering entire back of each head. Turn up brim on front of hat to just above eyes. Glue as needed to secure.

Pom-pom hats (make six): Sew long raw edges of six folded ribbing pieces together to make six tubes.

Tie a piece of thread tightly around short raw edge of each about 1/4 in. from edge. Turn each right side out. Hand-sew a white pom-pom to top of each hat.

Glue a hat onto each Santa with straight hair as directed above.

Fringed hats (make six): Sew long raw edges of remaining pieces of folded ribbing together to make six tubes.

Turn tubes right side out. Clip into raw edges of each to fringe ends, making 1/4-in.-long cuts about 1/4 in. apart.

Wrap a 14-in.-long piece of floss tightly around short raw edge of each about 1/2 in. from edge, and tie ends in a small bow opposite seam. Secure each bow with a bit of glue. Glue a green pom-pom to each end of each bow. Let dry.

Glue a hat onto each remaining Santa as directed above.

WOODEN GIFT BOXES: Drill an 1/8-in. hole through the center of each wooden cube.

Paint each cube red. When dry, apply varnish to each. Let dry.

Glue a piece of gold metallic ribbon around each cube without covering up

the holes. Let dry. Make 34 small bows from remaining ribbon. Glue a bow to each cube, covering ribbon ends on each. Let dry.

FINISHING: Tie a large knot in one end of white ribbon, leaving a 1-in. tail. Thread other end onto large hand-sewing needle.

String three green beads onto needle and slide beads to knotted end of ribbon. Then add a Santa head, piercing needle through back of hat near top of head, making sure Santa head remains in an upright position.

Add three green beads, a wooden gift box, three green beads and a different style Santa head.

Continue to add beads, wooden gift boxes and Santa heads, alternating styles of heads. After last Santa, add three beads and tie end of ribbon in a large knot close to last bead. Trim end of ribbon, leaving a 1-in. tail.

Hang up in your home! ☆

Gift-Giving Is in the Bag with This Easy Appliqued Tree Craft

RATHER than fuss with ribbons and wrapping paper, give Linda Whitener's handy fabric alternative a try. Her simple sack stitches up quickly…with long-lasting results.

Not only do small tokens fit inside, the bag can be re-used as a decoration or to hold potpourri. "It's also sized right to cover a box of tissues," notes the Glen Allen, Missouri crafter.

Materials Needed:
Tree pattern on this page
22-inch x 13-inch piece of red print
* for bag*
6-inch x 10-inch piece of green print
* for tree applique and bottom of bag*
Matching all-purpose thread
1/8 yard or scrap of paper-backed
* fusible web*
Buttons—three 3/8-inch clear and one
* 1/2-inch white*
3/4 yard of 1/8-inch-wide red satin
* ribbon*
Standard sewing supplies

Finished Size: Tree gift bag measures about 8 inches across x 8 inches tall.

Directions:
Trace tree pattern onto paper side of fusible web. Cut out tree, leaving a 1/2-in. margin on all sides.

Fuse tree to wrong side of green print, following manufacturer's directions. Cut out tree on traced lines.

Remove paper backing from tree. Center tree on right side of red print along 22-in. edge, with the bottom of the tree about 1 in. from one raw edge. Fuse tree in place.

Applique around tree with green thread and a medium satin stitch. Pull thread ends to wrong side and secure.

Hand-sew clear buttons randomly to

front of tree applique. Hand-sew white button to top of tree.

Fold red print fabric in half with right sides together to make an 11-in. x 13-in. piece. Sew 13-in. edges together with a 3/8-in. seam to make a gift bag. Press seam open.

From green print, cut a 5-3/4-in. square for bottom of gift bag.

Pin square to one raw edge of gift bag with right sides together and seam of bag centered along one edge and appliqued tree centered along opposite edge. Sew bottom in place with a 3/8-in. seam, leaving needle down at corners and turning fabric to make square corners. Clip corners.

For top hem and drawstring channel, fold remaining raw edge of gift bag 1/4 in. to wrong side and press. Fold same edge again 3 in. to wrong side for hem on top of bag and press.

Sew around top of bag close to first fold. Then sew around again 1/2 in. from first fold, sewing hem and outer fabric together to make a channel for ribbon. Turn gift bag right side out.

Snip into channel for ribbon at center front above tree applique, cutting through outside layer only. Thread ribbon through channel. Center ribbon and tie ends in overhand knots.

Tuck a token inside, then draw up ends of ribbon and tie in a small bow to close gift bag. Give to a friend! ☆

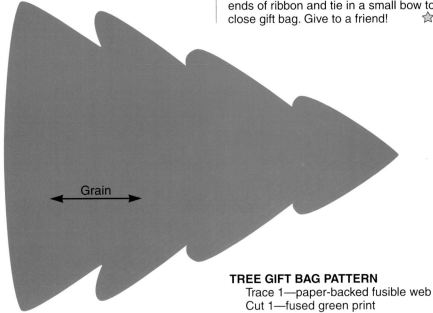

Grain

TREE GIFT BAG PATTERN
Trace 1—paper-backed fusible web
Cut 1—fused green print

Snowman Set Ices Nice Mealtime Look

TOP the table with this frosty runner and place mats designed by Jeanne Prue of Newport, Vermont…then get set for the compliments to pile high!

Materials Needed (for all):
Patterns on next page
Tracing paper and pencil
1/4 yard of paper-backed fusible web
Gold metallic or coordinating thread for quilting
Black six-strand embroidery floss
Embroidery needle
Quilter's ruler
Quilter's marking pen or pencil
Rotary cutter and mat (optional)
Standard sewing supplies

Materials Needed (for table runner):
44-inch-wide cotton or cotton-blend fabrics—1/4 yard each of green solid and white-on-white print for piecing; 1/2 yard of red solid for piecing, appliques and binding; 1/2 yard of unbleached muslin for backing; and 1/8 yard or scrap of black solid for hat applique
Matching all-purpose thread
14-inch x 38-inch piece of lightweight quilt batting

Materials Needed (for each place mat):
44-inch-wide cotton or cotton-blend fabrics—1/8 yard of white-on-white print for piecing; 1/4 yard each of red solid and green solid for piecing, appliques and binding; 1/2 yard each of light green print for center and unbleached muslin for backing; and 1/8 yard or scrap of black solid for hat applique
Matching all-purpose thread
14-inch x 22-inch piece of lightweight quilt batting

Finished Size: Table runner is 12-1/2 inches wide x 36-1/2 inches long. Each place mat measures 20-1/2 inches wide x 12-1/2 inches high.

Directions:
Pre-wash all fabrics without fabric softeners, washing colors separately. If the water from any fabric is discolored, wash again until rinse water runs clear. Machine-dry and press all fabrics.

Cut fabrics using rotary cutter and quilter's ruler or mark fabrics using ruler and marker and cut with scissors.

Do all piecing with right sides of fabrics together and 1/4-in. seams. Press seams toward darker fabric unless oth-

erwise directed.

TABLE RUNNER: Cutting: From red solid, cut three 2-1/4-in. x 42-in. crosswise strips for binding. For piecing, cut eight 2-7/8-in. squares and four 4-7/8-in. squares. Also cut eight 2-1/2-in. x 4-1/2-in. rectangles for piecing.

From green solid, cut four 4-7/8-in. squares. Also cut four 2-1/2-in. x 4-1/2-in. rectangles and three 4-1/2-in. squares.

From white-on-white print, cut eight 2-7/8-in. squares. Also cut twelve 2-1/2-in. x 4-1/2-in. rectangles.

Applique: Trace individual snowman patterns onto paper side of fusible web and mitten pattern onto tracing paper as directed on patterns, leaving a 1/2-in. margin between shapes. Trace mitten pattern onto paper side of fusible web twice. Reverse pattern and trace two more onto paper side of fusible web. Cut shapes apart.

Fuse shapes to wrong side of fabrics as directed on patterns, following manufacturer's directions. Cut out shapes on traced lines.

Remove paper backing from each shape. Fuse two mittens onto right side of a 4-1/2-in. green solid square with thumbs facing as shown in photo. Repeat, using remaining mittens and another 4-1/2-in. green solid square.

Fuse snowman shapes onto right side of remaining 4-1/2-in. green solid square as shown on pattern.

Applique around mittens with matching thread and a medium satin stitch.

Applique around snowman shapes with a medium satin stitch in the follow-

ing order: With white thread, stitch around head. Then stitch around hat with black thread. Use red thread to stitch around hatband and nose.

Pull all thread ends to wrong side and secure.

Separate six-strand floss and use three strands to stem-stitch mouth where shown on pattern. Use two strands to stitch the two French knot eyes where shown on pattern. See Fig. 1 for stitch illustrations.

Piecing: Cut red and green 4-7/8-in. squares in half diagonally to make eight red and eight green triangles.

Sew a red triangle to each green triangle along long matched edges to make eight red and green pieced triangle squares. Trim each to make an accurate 4-1/2-in. square.

Cut red and white-on-white print 2-7/8-in. squares in half diagonally to make 16 red and 16 white triangles. Sew a red triangle to each white triangle along long matched edges to make 16 red and white pieced triangle squares.

Sew four red and white pieced triangle squares together as shown in Fig. 2 to make a pieced red and white pinwheel block. Repeat, making a total of four. Evenly trim each side to make an accurate 4-1/2-in. square.

Sew a white-on-white print 2-1/2-in. x 4-1/2-in. rectangle with long edges matching to each red solid and each green solid 2-1/2-in. x 4-1/2-in. rectangle to make eight red and white pieced squares and four green and white pieced squares. Evenly trim each side to make an accurate 4-1/2-in. square.

Assembly: Lay out all pieced and appliqued blocks as shown in Table Runner Assembly Diagram.

Sew all blocks together as nine-patch blocks. Sew blocks together to make rows. Then sew rows together as shown in Assembly Diagram.

Stitch end blocks to the center block as shown in Assembly Diagram.

Quilting: Cut a 14-in. x 38-in. piece of muslin for backing. Place backing wrong side up on a flat surface and smooth out wrinkles. Place batting centered over backing and smooth out. Center pieced table runner right side up over batting and smooth out.

Hand-baste through all three layers, stitching from center to corners, then horizontally and vertically every 4 in. until layers are securely held together.

Machine-quilt with gold metallic thread or coordinating quilting thread, stitching in the ditch of seams joining pieced and appliqued blocks.

Trim batting and backing even with edges of pieced table runner.

Binding: Stitch the short ends of red solid binding strips together to make one long strip. Fold binding in half lengthwise with wrong sides together and press.

Pin binding to right side of table runner, matching raw edges. Beginning with a 1/4-in. fold to the wrong side, stitch binding to table runner with a 1/4-in. seam, mitering corners. Overlap ends of binding and trim excess.

Fold binding to back of table runner, covering seam. Baste or pin to hold. Machine-stitch with matching thread, stitching through binding close to seam on right side and catching fold on back of table runner.

PLACE MAT: Cutting: From white-on-white print, cut eight 2-7/8-in. squares for piecing.

From red solid, cut two 2-1/4-in. x 42-in. crosswise strips for binding and eight 2-7/8-in. squares for piecing.

From green solid, cut two 4-1/2-in. squares for blocks.

From light green print, cut one 12-1/2-in. square for center.

Applique: Follow instructions for table runner to make one appliqued mitten block and one snowman block.

Piecing: Cut red solid and white-on-white print 2-7/8-in. squares in half diagonally to make 16 red and 16 white triangles. Sew a red triangle to each white triangle along long matched edges to make 16 pieced triangle squares.

Sew four red and white pieced triangle squares together as shown in Fig. 2 to make a pinwheel block. Repeat, making a total of four. Trim each to make an

accurate 4-1/2-in. square.

Assembly: Lay out pieced blocks and light green print center block as shown in Place Mat Assembly Diagram.

Sew the snowman block and mitten block between two pinwheel blocks for ends of place mat. Then sew pieced end with snowman to left side of center and

pieced end with mittens to right side.

Quilting: Cut a 14-in. x 22-in. piece of muslin for backing.

Quilt as directed in table runner quilting instructions.

Binding: Bind place mat as directed in table runner binding instructions.

Set your Christmastime table! ☆

SNOWMAN TABLE RUNNER AND PLACE MAT PATTERNS

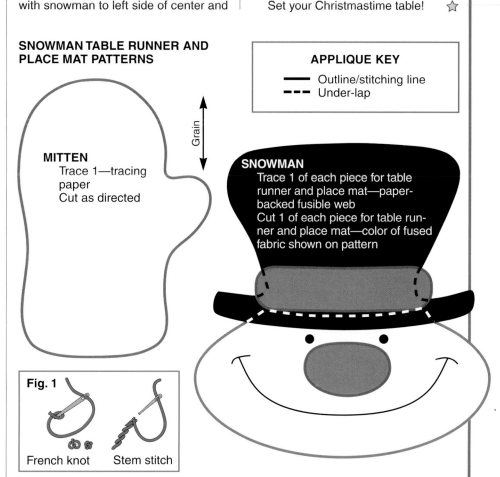

APPLIQUE KEY

—— Outline/stitching line

- - - Under-lap

MITTEN
Trace 1—tracing paper
Cut as directed

Grain

SNOWMAN
Trace 1 of each piece for table runner and place mat—paper-backed fusible web
Cut 1 of each piece for table runner and place mat—color of fused fabric shown on pattern

Fig. 1

French knot   Stem stitch

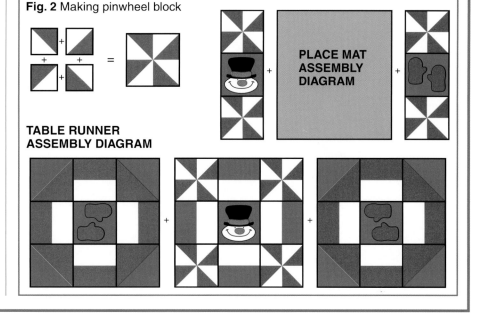

Fig. 2 Making pinwheel block

PLACE MAT ASSEMBLY DIAGRAM

TABLE RUNNER ASSEMBLY DIAGRAM

Snowy Shawl Wraps Up Comfort

EVEN if the weather outside is frightful, this fluffy knit wrap is just delightful, assures Rebecca Pena of Walpole, New Hampshire.

"It's perfect for cuddling up with a good book…yet pretty enough to wear to church on chilly mornings," she notes. "And if you're making it as a gift, you don't have to worry about getting the size right."

Rebecca used a mohair-like yarn to give her shawl extra softness, but any kind of 4-ply yarn will do.

Materials Needed:
10 ounces of 4-ply white yarn
Size 13 knitting needles
Size K/10-1/2 (6.5mm) crochet hook

Gauge: 6 sts and 10 rows = 2 inches.

Finished Size: Triangular shawl measures about 72 inches across x 30 inches high.

Directions:
SHAWL: Cast on 5 sts.

Row 1: K 2, inc 1 st in the next st, k 2: 6 sts.
Rows 2-4: K 1, inc 1, k across row to last st, inc 1, k 1.
Row 5: K across row.
Repeat Rows 2-5 until there are 150 sts on your needle.
Knit each row for 2-1/2 inches: 150 sts. Bind off loosely.
FRINGE: Add fringe to the end of every row and to center of Row 1.
For each fringe, cut four 9-in. lengths of yarn. Hold the four strands together as one and fold them in half.
Insert the crochet hook in a stitch at the end of a row and catch the fold of the yarn pieces. Pull the fold through the stitch just enough to form a loop. Then draw the yarn ends through loop and pull ends to tighten loop.
Model your cozy country shawl! ☆

ABBREVIATIONS	
inc	increase
k	knit
st(s)	stitch(es)

Festive Foam Tags Tie on Good Cheer

HERE'S a can-do craft you won't want to put a lid on! The merry tie-ons from Verlyn King of Tremonton, Utah will wrap up everything from jars of treats to evergreen boughs and wrapped packages with style.

Speeding the project along is the material they are cut from—sturdy quick-to-snip craft foam. "You could also use felt to create softer versions that are just as fast," Verlyn advises.

Materials Needed (for all):
Patterns on next page
Tracing paper and pencil
Plastic craft foam—3/4-inch square of brown, 1-1/2-inch square of flesh, 5-inch x 8-inch piece of green, 3-inch x 6-inch piece of red, 4-inch square of white and 1-3/4-inch square of yellow
Two 7mm glue-on wiggle eyes
1/4-inch round hole punch
1/8-inch-wide satin ribbon—1/2 yard of

yellow and 1 yard of red
Low-temperature glue gun and
  glue sticks
*Sharpie black fine-point permanent
  marker (or other brand that won't
  rub off foam)*
Scissors

Finished Size: Santa is 4-1/2 inches tall
x 2-1/2 inches wide. Tree is 4-1/2 inches tall x 3-3/4 inches wide. Wreath is
about 3-1/2 inches across.

Directions:
CUTTING: Trace individual pattern
pieces onto tracing paper as directed on
patterns. Cut out shapes on traced
lines. Use pencil to trace outlines of
each onto back of color of craft foam
shown on patterns. Cut out shapes on
traced lines.

   ASSEMBLY: Santa: Glue white
beard to bottom edge of hat. Do not
overlap pieces. When dry, glue hat and
beard over 1-1/2-in. flesh square for
Santa's face. Glue pom-pom to top of hat
and hatband over joined hat and beard
where shown on pattern.

   Use hole punch to make two holes

in top of hat as shown on pattern. Keep
one punched red circle for Santa's nose.

   Glue nose and wiggle eyes to Santa's
face where indicated on pattern.

   Thread ends of an 18-in. length of red
ribbon from front to back through holes
in Santa's hat.

   Tree: Glue star to top of tree and trunk
to bottom as shown on patterns.

   Use hole punch to make holes in star
where indicated on pattern. Also punch
seven circles from scraps of red foam.
Glue circles to tree for trims.

   Thread ends of yellow ribbon from
front to back through holes in star.

   Wreath: Glue red bow to top of
wreath where indicated on pattern.

   Use hole punch to make holes in
bow where indicated on pattern. Also
make seven additional red circles
from scraps of foam for berries and
glue to wreath.

   Thread ends of an 18-in. length of
red ribbon from back to front through
holes in bow. Tie ends in a bow on front
of wreath.

   FINISHING: Use marker to write "To:"
and "From:" on back of each gift tag.

   Tie tags onto goody-filled jars! ☆

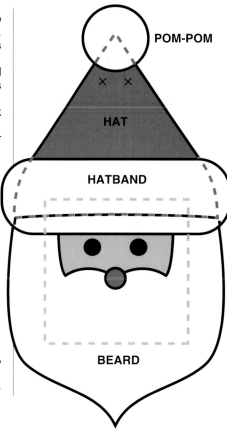

POM-POM

HAT

HATBAND

BEARD

FOAM JAR TRIM PATTERNS
   Trace 1 each piece—tracing paper
   Cut 1 each piece—color of craft foam shown
   X = punched hole

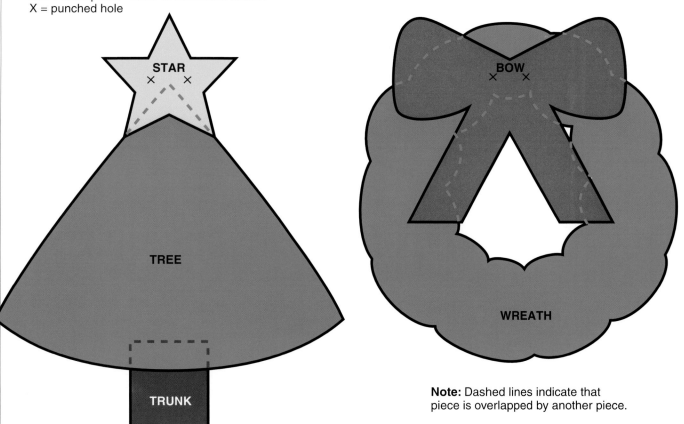

STAR

TREE

TRUNK

BOW

WREATH

Note: Dashed lines indicate that
piece is overlapped by another piece.

Simple Trims Send Noel Message

CHALKING it up to her love for the season, Mary Ayres crafted a trio of trims for her Christmas tree using mini slates and craft sticks.

"I had the wooden ovals on hand and with some creative painting and enhancing, I came up with this festive Santa, reindeer and angel," she confides from her Boyce, Virginia home.

Materials Needed (for each):
2-inch x 3-inch mini chalkboard
Three craft sticks
1/16-inch-thick x 2-inch-long wooden oval shape for head
Paper plate or palette
Paper towels
Small container of water
Paintbrushes—small flat and small round
Black fine-line permanent marker
White (tacky) glue
Ruler
Pencil
8 inches of gold metallic thread for hanger

Materials Needed (for Santa):
1/4-inch white pom-pom for hat
Acrylic craft paints—black, flesh, red and white

Materials Needed (for angel):
Two 1/16-inch-thick x 1-1/2-inch-high wooden heart shapes for wings
Craft pick or flat toothpick for halo
Acrylic craft paints—flesh, light gold, red, white and gold metallic

Materials Needed (for reindeer):
Six craft picks or three flat toothpicks for antlers
Two 1/16-inch-thick x 7/8-inch-long wooden teardrop shapes for ears
Acrylic craft paints—brown, red, tan and white
1/4-inch red pom-pom for nose

Finished Size: Angel and Santa trims are 5-1/4 inches tall x 4-1/2 inches across. Reindeer trim is 6 inches tall x 4-1/2 inches across.

Directions:
Place small amounts of paints as needed onto paper plate or palette. Add additional coats of paint as needed for complete coverage, allowing drying time between each coat. Extend paint onto side edges of pieces.

For each trim, glue a craft stick centered to the top front of one long edge of one chalkboard. Glue a craft stick to back of each short edge of chalkboard, leaving about 2-1/2 in. of each craft stick exposed for legs as shown in photo.

SANTA: Use pencil to draw Santa's face freehand as shown in Painting Diagram onto one side of an oval wood piece.

Use flat brush and flesh to paint Santa's face onto oval and hands at ends of top craft stick.

When completely dry, use flat brush and white to paint Santa's beard and mustache and the fur trim on his hat, legs and arms. Use round brush to add white lettering to the chalkboard as shown in the photo. Let dry.

Use flat brush to paint about 1/2 in. of end of each leg black for Santa's boots.

Use flat brush to paint frame and backs of chalkboard and craft sticks red. When dry, paint fronts of craft sticks and Santa's hat red as shown. Let dry.

Use black marker to outline fur trim, beard and mustache.

Dip flat brush into red and wipe off excess paint until no brush strokes show. Use circular motion to add cheeks to face.

Glue pom-pom to left edge of hat. Glue head centered along top craft stick.

ANGEL: Use a pencil to draw the angel's face freehand as shown in the Painting Diagram onto one side of an oval wood piece.

Referring to photo for placement, use flat brush and light gold to paint arms and shoes. Then paint frame and back of chalkboard light gold. When dry, paint legs, hands and face flesh. Let dry.

Use flat brush to paint all sides of each heart white. Use round brush and white to add lettering to chalkboard as shown in photo. Let dry.

Use flat brush to add gold metallic highlights to rounded portion of each heart for wings.

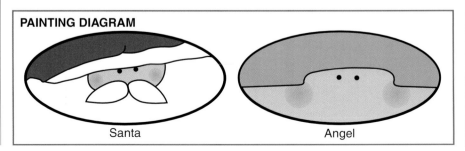

PAINTING DIAGRAM

Santa

Angel

Cut a 2-1/4-in. piece from craft stick or toothpick for halo. Use flat brush to paint halo metallic gold. Let dry.

Glue head centered along top craft stick and halo to front of head. Glue hearts to back of chalkboard with points facing the center back and round portions exposed for wings.

Use black marker to outline hair, hands and ties of shoes. Add small dots for eyes.

Dip flat brush into red and wipe off excess paint until no brush strokes show. Use circular motion to add cheeks to face.

REINDEER: Use flat brush and tan to paint all sides of an oval for head and two teardrop shapes for ears. Also paint frame and back of chalkboard and craft sticks tan. Let dry.

Use round brush and white to add lettering to chalkboard as shown in photo. Let dry.

Cut two 1-1/4-in.-long pieces from pointed ends of craft picks or toothpicks for antlers. Cut four 3/4-in.-long pieces from remaining pointed ends of craft picks or toothpicks.

Glue two short pieces to back of each long piece as shown in photo. When dry, paint antlers brown. Let dry.

Glue antlers and teardrops for ears to the back of one long side of oval as shown in photo. Glue head centered along top craft stick.

Use marker to add two small eyes.

Dip flat brush into red and wipe off excess paint until no brush strokes show. Use circular motion to add cheeks.

Glue pom-pom to lower edge of oval for nose.

FINISHING: Tie ends of each piece of gold metallic thread together in an overhand knot to make loops for hangers. Glue knot centered to back of each chalkboard.

Hang trims from tree branches or use as package toppers! ☆

Angels Are Ingrained with Spirit

POISED to bring the true meaning of Christmas to the season are these pretty cherubs…and you can easily help them take wing!

Sheila Divvens of West Melbourne, Florida offers the instructions for making the angels from wood, dried flowers and paper twist. She adds that they're fun and simple enough for both beginners and more experienced crafters to try.

Materials Needed (for each):

1-3/4-inch-wide x 6-1/2-inch-long piece of 1-inch-thick pine
1/4-inch-thick slice from 1-inch-diameter dowel for head
Scroll or band saw

Fig. 1 Cutting stick angel

Side view

Top

Front

Back 6-1/2 in.

Bottom

1 in.

Sandpaper and tack cloth
9-1/2 inches of 4-inch-wide paper twist in color of choice
Coordinating small ribbon rose or dried flowers
12 inches of 1/8-inch-wide coordinating satin ribbon
Brown wood stain and soft cloth
10 inches of 2-ply jute string
Dried Spanish moss
Glue gun and glue stick
Scissors

Finished Size: Each angel is about 5 inches across x 7 inches high, excluding hanger.

Directions:
With 1-in. side of pine facing up, cut diagonally from one corner to opposite corner to make a tapered wedge for angel's body. See Fig. 1.

Cut off 1/2 in. from narrow end to make body 6 in. long.

Lightly sand all wood pieces and wipe with tack cloth. Apply stain to wood pieces with soft cloth. Let dry.

Bring ends of jute string together and glue them to one flat side of dowel piece for hanger. Then glue dowel piece with ends of jute string sandwiched in between to top front of body for head.

Glue Spanish moss to top, sides and back of head around hanging loop.

Cut a 4-in.-long piece of paper twist. Untwist paper twist and cut it in half lengthwise. Discard one piece. Fold the remaining piece in thirds lengthwise, forming narrow 4-in.-long arms. Twist arms once in center to shape hands. Glue ends to back of angel's body about

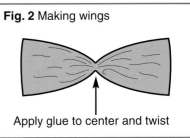

Fig. 2 Making wings

Apply glue to center and twist

1/2 in. below head.

Cut a 5-1/2-in.-long piece of paper twist. Untwist paper twist and trim ends square. Place a bead of glue down the center and twist paper in center to form wings. See Fig. 2. Let dry.

Glue twisted center of wings to back of angel's body, covering ends of arms.

Glue ribbon rose or dried flowers to center front over twist of hands. Tie ribbon into a small bow and glue bow to angel as shown in photo. Trim ribbon ends to desired length.

Spread good cheer by adding an angel to a gift basket or stocking! ☆

Old-Fashioned Santa Claus Will Greet Yule with Open Arms...

POSE this well-seasoned fellow on a shelf or counter and get set to see some cheery looks! The cone-shaped jolly old elf is a cinch to assemble from scraps, according to designer Karen Wittkop of Duluth, Minnesota.

Materials Needed:

Patterns on this page and the next page
Tracing paper and pencil
12-inch square of red and green plaid fabric
5-inch square of off-white felt for beard and mustache
1-1/2-inch square of off-white fabric for face
10-1/2-inch-long x 1-1/4-inch-wide piece of off-white fake fur
3-inch circle of cardboard
Polyester fiberfill
4 inches of jute string
6mm jingle bell
Two round 3mm black beads for eyes
1/2 cup of cinnamon
1/4 cup of applesauce
Rolling pin
Waxed paper
Paper towels
Table knife

White (tacky) glue
Acrylic craft paints—green, red and white
1/8-inch-wide satin ribbon—6 inches each of green and white
1/2 yard of white or white and red metallic crochet thread
Glue gun and glue sticks
Standard sewing supplies

Finished Size: Santa is 9 inches tall x 3-3/4 inches across.

Directions:

GINGERBREAD MEN: Mix together 1/3 cup cinnamon, 1/4 cup applesauce and 3/4 tablespoon tacky glue.

Knead ingredients together, adding more cinnamon if needed to make a stiff dough. Coat work surface and rolling pin with remaining cinnamon and roll out dough to 1/4-in. thickness.

Trace gingerbread pattern onto waxed paper twice and cut out each along traced lines.

Place gingerbread patterns on dough and cut out with table knife. Transfer gingerbread shapes onto paper towels and allow to dry on a flat surface overnight or until firm.

When dry, use toothpick dipped in white paint to add eyes, one button, and white dots around hands and feet as shown on pattern. In the same way, add red dot for mouth and red and green but-

tons to each. Let dry.

SANTA: Mark tracing paper with a 1-in. grid. Draw cone pattern onto tracing paper as shown.

Trace remaining patterns onto tracing paper and cut out.

Cut cone, arms, beard, mustache and face from fabrics as directed on patterns. From fur, cut one 10-1/2-in. x 3/4-in. strip and one 3-1/2-in. x 1/2-in. strip.

Pin two arm pieces right sides together with edges matching and stitch around curved edge with 1/4-in. seam, leaving short straight edge open. Repeat with two remaining arm pieces.

Turn arms right side out and stuff firmly. Turn in raw edges 1/4 in. and hand-stitch openings closed.

Fold cone piece with right sides together and long straight edges matching. Stitch long straight edges together from wide to narrow end with 1/4-in. seam, leaving bottom edge open. Turn right side out and stuff firmly.

Hand-stitch 1/4 in. from edge around opening using a running stitch and leaving a tail of thread. See Fig. 1 for stitch illustration.

Place cardboard circle inside fabric cone over stuffing. Pull thread, drawing about 1/2 in. of fabric around cardboard circle. Fasten and clip thread.

Apply glue to wrong side of face. Glue face to cone opposite seam with

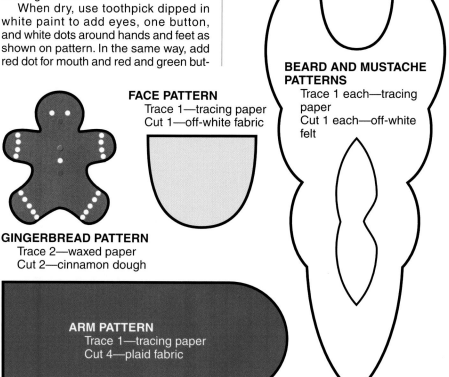

FACE PATTERN
Trace 1—tracing paper
Cut 1—off-white fabric

BEARD AND MUSTACHE PATTERNS
Trace 1 each—tracing paper
Cut 1 each—off-white felt

GINGERBREAD PATTERN
Trace 2—waxed paper
Cut 2—cinnamon dough

ARM PATTERN
Trace 1—tracing paper
Cut 4—plaid fabric

straight edge 2-1/2 in. from tip of cone.

Glue beard onto face, matching straight edges of face and beard. Glue mustache to beard and eyes to face.

Glue 3-1/2-in. fur strip around cone over top edge of beard and face, with ends meeting at seam of cone. Glue remaining fur strip to bottom of cone, with ends meeting at seam. Trim ends as needed.

Glue arms to body 3-1/2 in. from point, with straight edges 1/2 in. from seam.

FINISHING: Cut a 4-in. piece of jute and glue an end to each hand. Glue ginger-

bread cutouts to jute.

Tie ribbons into small bows and glue to gingerbread cutouts.

Wrap each arm with a piece of crochet thread about 1 in. from end. Knot

and trim ends 1/4 in. from knot. Make a small bow with remaining thread and glue bow to tip of cone.

Glue jingle bell to tip of cone. Stand Santa on a shelf! ☆

Fig. 1 Running stitch

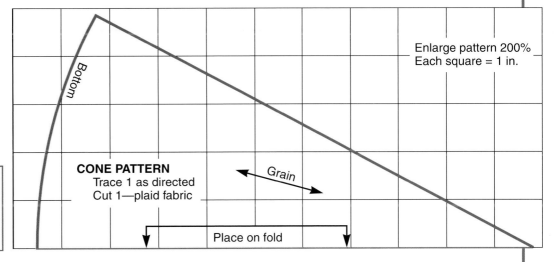

CONE PATTERN
Trace 1 as directed
Cut 1—plaid fabric

Grain

Enlarge pattern 200%
Each square = 1 in.

Bottom

Place on fold

Accent's Abloom for the Holidays

TO PERK UP your home, try planting this festive flower all around. You can arrange several on a wreath like we did here, or use blooms to brighten centerpieces, swags and the Christmas tree!

Crafter Muriel O'Brien from Washington, Michigan shares the easy-to-grow know-how below.

Materials Needed (for each):
3-inch-wide velvet ribbon—24 inches of red and 8 inches of green
Matching thread and hand-sewing needle
20 inches of 3/4-inch-wide gold metallic ribbon
Pencil or pen
Ruler
26-gauge craft wire
Floral tape
Wire cutters
Scissors

Finished Size: Each poinsettia trim is about 7-1/2 inches long x 3 inches high.

Directions:
Place green ribbon wrong side up on a flat surface. Measure and mark 5-1/2 in. from one end along bottom edge of ribbon. From same end, measure and mark 2-1/4 in. and 7-3/4 in. on top edge of ribbon.

Draw a line to connect lower corner on bottom of ribbon to 2-1/4-in. mark on top of ribbon. Then draw a line connecting 5-1/2-in. mark on bottom of ribbon to 7-3/4-in. mark on top of ribbon. See Fig. 1. Cut on marked lines.

Use green ribbon for pattern and cut three pieces of red ribbon in same way.

Fold each ribbon in half crosswise and crease fold to mark stitching line.

Thread needle with double strand of matching thread. Hand-sew a running stitch on stitching line of one ribbon. See Fig. 1 above left for stitch illustration. Draw up thread to gather and fasten off. Repeat, using remaining ribbon pieces.

Cut gold metallic ribbon into five 4-in.-long pieces. Tie an overhand knot in center of each length of ribbon.

Bring ends of ribbon down, leaving knot on top, and wrap a 12-in.-long piece of craft wire around ends just below knot. Add remaining knotted ribbons one at a time in the same way, then coil the rest of the wire around the ribbon ends.

Cut five 6-in.-long pieces of craft wire. Wrap center of a piece of wire around center of each gathered ribbon and twist ends together in back.

Place a red ribbon on top of green ribbon and wire ends together. Then add the gold ribbon bunch and twist wire ends together as one. Add remaining red ribbons one at a time, twisting wire

ends together after each addition. Wire entire group together, shaping ribbons as shown in photo. Wrap exposed wires with floral tape.

If desired, wire onto an artificial wreath as shown above. ☆

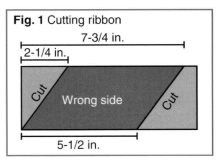

Fig. 1 Cutting ribbon

7-3/4 in.

2-1/4 in.

Cut

Wrong side

Cut

5-1/2 in.

Patchwork Skirt Rings Fir Festively

YOU'LL ROUND UP a notable Noel when you drape the base of your Christmas tree with this colorful scalloped cover-up from designer Donna Stefanik of Westfield, Massachusetts.

Keeping the skirt in tune with the season are the heart appliques and jingle bells that dress up the center. "Any motif could be stitched on," counsels Donna. "Instead of bells, buttons or bows make nice attachments, too."

Materials Needed:

Patterns on this page and the next page
Tracing paper and pencil
44-inch-wide 100% cotton fabrics—1/3 yard each of four different Christmas prints for pieced edging; eight 5-inch squares of several different Christmas prints for heart appliques; and 4 yards of red solid for center sections and backing
Matching all-purpose thread
44-inch square of lightweight quilt batting
Quilter's marking pen or pencil
Quilter's ruler
Seven 3/4-inch gold jingle bells
Standard sewing supplies

Finished Size: Tree skirt measures about 42 inches across.

Directions:

Pre-wash fabrics, washing each color separately. If the water from any fabric is discolored, wash again until rinse water runs clear. Dry and press all fabrics.

Do all piecing with accurate 1/4-in. seams and right sides of fabrics together. Press seams toward darker fabric when possible.

CUTTING: Mark tracing paper with a 1-in. grid. Draw patterns A, B, C, D and E onto tracing paper as shown on the pattern, leaving a 1-in. margin between shapes. Cut out patterns, adding a 1/4-in. seam allowance on outside edges of each pattern.

Trace the heart pattern onto tracing paper as shown. Cut out the heart, adding a 1/4-in. seam allowance.

Placing patterns A, B, C and D on right side of different fabrics, cut eight each from four different Christmas prints for pieced edging.

Placing pattern E on the right side of the red solid, cut eight for center sections.

Cut eight hearts from several different Christmas prints.

PIECING: Sew Edgings A, B, C and D together as shown on pattern. Repeat, making a total of eight pieced edgings.

Sew the top edge of a pieced edging to the bottom edge of center section E to make a pieced center section. Clip curve and press seam toward pieced edging. Repeat, making a total of eight pieced center sections.

Sew the long edges of eight pieced center sections together, stitching seven seams and leaving two seam allowances unstitched for center back opening of tree skirt.

APPLIQUE: Turn 1/4 in. to wrong side of each heart and press.

Place a heart centered about 1-1/2 in. above pieced edging on each section

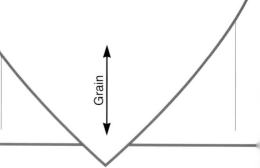

HEART
Trace 1—tracing paper
Cut 8—several different
Christmas prints

Grain

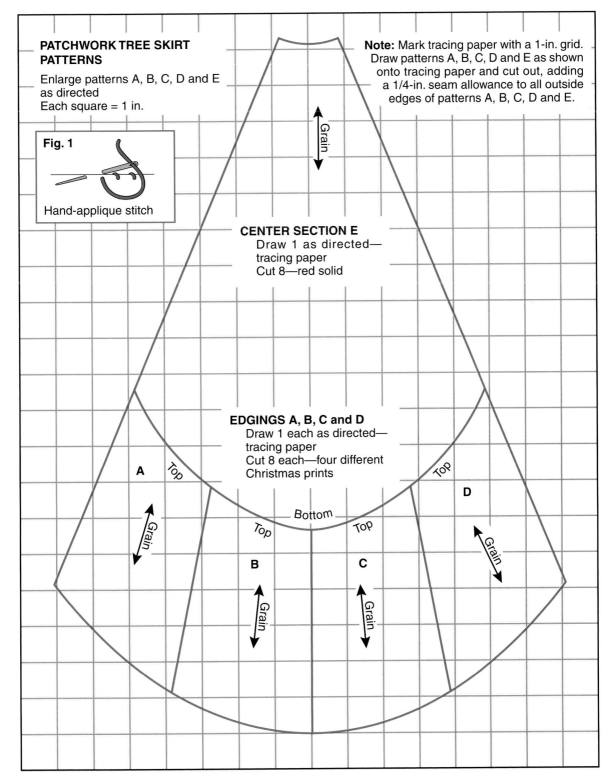

PATCHWORK TREE SKIRT PATTERNS

Enlarge patterns A, B, C, D and E as directed
Each square = 1 in.

Fig. 1

Hand-applique stitch

Note: Mark tracing paper with a 1-in. grid. Draw patterns A, B, C, D and E as shown onto tracing paper and cut out, adding a 1/4-in. seam allowance to all outside edges of patterns A, B, C, D and E.

Grain

CENTER SECTION E
Draw 1 as directed—
tracing paper
Cut 8—red solid

EDGINGS A, B, C and D
Draw 1 each as directed—
tracing paper
Cut 8 each—four different
Christmas prints

A

Top

Top

D

Top

Bottom

Grain

Top

Top

B

C

Grain

Grain

Grain

of tree skirt as shown in photo.

Hand-applique hearts to tree skirt using matching thread. See Fig. 1 for stitch illustration.

ASSEMBLY: Place batting on a flat surface and smooth out wrinkles. Center backing fabric right side up on top of batting and smooth. Center pieced tree skirt over backing, wrong side up, and smooth. Pin to hold. Trim batting and backing even with pieced top.

Sew all layers together, stitching 1/4 in. from outside edges of pieced tree skirt and leaving an opening along one straight edge for turning. Clip curves and trim corners. Turn right side out through opening. Turn raw edges of opening in and hand-sew opening closed.

Hand-sew a jingle bell to pieced edging at each section seam.

Wrap around the Christmas tree. ☆

Cherubs Tune in to Noel Meaning

CREATING a happy harmonious atmosphere is what these musically inclined Christmas angels are designed to do—as they're enhancing branches, prettily wrapped presents and more!

Penny Duff of Kennebunk, Maine assures that her cross-stitch cherubs are almost effortless to make. "They work up quickly," she smiles, "and you can choose any hues you like."

Materials Needed (for both):

Charts on this page
Four 4-inch x 4-1/2-inch pieces of white 18-count Aida cloth
DMC six-strand embroidery floss in
colors listed on color key
Kreinik metallic blending filament in color listed on color key
Small amount of polyester stuffing
Size 26 tapestry needle
White all-purpose thread
Standard sewing supplies

Finished Size: Each tree trim is 3-1/2 inches wide x 3 inches high. The Design area of each is 54 stitches wide x 43 stitches high.

Directions:

Zigzag or overcast edges of two 4-in. x 4-1/2-in. pieces of Aida cloth to prevent fraying. Fold each in half lengthwise and then in half crosswise to determine center and mark this point.

To find center of charts, draw lines across charts connecting arrows. Begin stitching each at this point so designs will be centered.

Working with 18-in. lengths of six-strand floss, separate strands and use two strands for cross-stitching and one strand for backstitching. Use four strands of blending filament for cross-stitching. See Fig. 1 for stitch illustrations.

Each square on the chart is equal to one stitch worked over a set of fabric threads. Use the colors indicated on

CROSS-STITCHED ANGELS	
COLOR KEY	**DMC**
☐ Ecru	
△ Light Pink	224
■ Red	304
▣ Dark Green	501
▨ Medium Green	502
▥ Light Tan	543
☐ Gold	680
● Dark Red	815
◉ Dark Blue	930
☐ Peach	951
BACKSTITCHING	
— Dark Green	501
— Medium Green	502
— Dark Red	815
— Dark Brown	938
BLENDING FILAMENT	**Kreinik**
☒ Gold Metallic	002

BELL ANGEL CHART　　　　　　　　**TRUMPET ANGEL CHART**

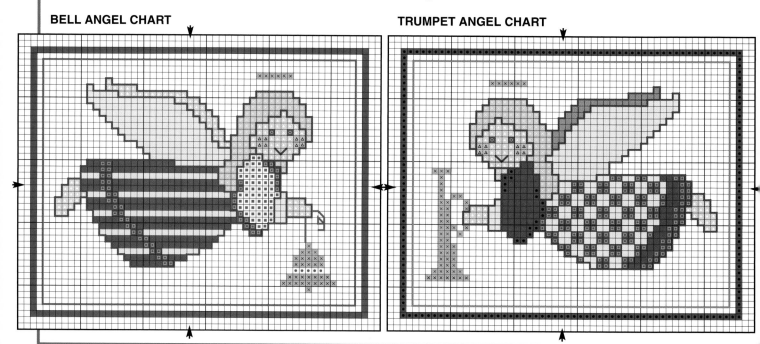

the color key to complete cross-stitching, then backstitching.

Do not knot floss on back of work. Instead, leave a short tail of floss on back of work and hold it in place while working the first few stitches over it. To end a strand, run needle under a few neighboring stitches in back before cutting floss close to work.

When stitching is completed, and only if necessary, wash gently in lukewarm water. Press right side down on terry towel to dry.

FINISHING: Pin one unstitched piece of Aida cloth to the back of one stitched piece with outside edges matching.

Machine-stitch the two layers together, stitching one square outside border of stitched design and leaving a small opening for stuffing. Stuff lightly and stitch the opening closed. Repeat for the other design.

Trim outside edges of each design five squares from stitching. To fringe edges, remove threads from Aida cloth to one square from stitching.

Sew a 7-in. length of gold blending filament to back at top corners of each trim to make a hanging loop.

Display your angels! ☆

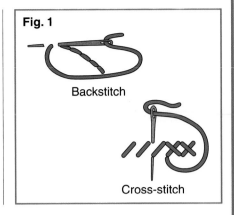

Fig. 1

Backstitch

Cross-stitch

Cover Bundles Season in Cozy Country Style

BLANKET your home in holiday hues with this cheerful crocheted coverlet from Helle Hill of Thornton, Colorado. "The afghan really 'says' Christmas at our house," she smiles.

The country crafter relied on easy-to-find worsted-weight yarn and simple stitches to make her lap-size afghan. Like a larger version for your bed? Just add more rows!

Materials Needed:
4-ply worsted-weight yarn—two 8-ounce skeins each of green, red and white (Helle used Red Heart Super Saver yarn in Soft White, Cherry Red and Paddy Green)
Size F/5 (3.75mm) crochet hook or size needed to obtain correct gauge
Tapestry needle
Scissors

Gauge: Each stitch group is approximately 1 inch long x 3/4 inch high. Slight variations in gauge will not affect this project.

Finished Size: Afghan is about 32 inches wide x 36 inches long.

Directions:
With red, ch 143.

Row 1: Dc in fourth ch from hk, hdc in next ch, sc in next ch, sl st in next ch (counts as first group); * ch 3, dc in next

ch, hdc in next ch, sc in next ch, sl st in next ch (counts as each additional group); repeat from * across to end of ch, turn: 35 groups.

Row 2: Ch 3, sl st in first ch-3 sp, ch 3, work 3 dcs in same ch-3 sp (counts as first group); * sl st in next ch-3 sp, ch 3, work 3 dcs in same ch-3 sp (counts as each additional group); repeat from * across, working ending repeat in beginning ch-3 sp of previous row, turn: 35 groups.

Rows 3-4: Repeat Row 2. Fasten off at end of Row 4.

Rows 5-8: Attach green and repeat Row 2. Fasten off at end of Row 8.

Rows 9-12: Attach white and repeat Row 2. Fasten off at end of Row 12.

Rows 13-16: Attach red and repeat Row 2. Fasten off at end of Row 16.

Repeat Rows 5-16 until you have used each color a total of seven times.

Use the tapestry needle to weave in all loose ends.

Snuggle up under your afghan! ☆

ABBREVIATIONS

ch(s)	chain(s)
dc(s)	double crochet(s)
hdc(s)	half double crochet(s)
hk	hook
sc(s)	single crochet(s)
sl st	slip stitch
sp(s)	space(es)
*	Instructions following asterisk are repeated as instructed.

Basket Brims with Fun Trims

HERE'S a project that will set a cheerful Christmas scene in mere moments! Designer Janna Britton of Firebaugh, California points out that her plastic canvas basket trims can easily accent almost any container.

"Wooden boxes and tins are other options," she suggests. "Or add a magnet to each shape to create fridgies."

Materials Needed:
Charts on this page and the next page
Plastic canvas—3-1/2-inch x 4-inch piece of 10-count white for roof, candy canes and door; 3-1/2-inch square of 14-count clear or brown for house; and 5-inch x 9-inch piece of 7-count clear or green for trees
Six-strand embroidery floss—8 yards each of white and light brown and 1 yard of green
Six-strand rayon embroidery floss—8 yards of white
Metallic thread—5 yards of red and 3 yards of gold (Janna used Kreinik medium braid in Red 003HL and Kreinik Facets thread in Antique Gold)
4-ply worsted-weight yarn—40 yards of light green and 3 yards of dark green

Tapestry needle
1-3/4-inch-tall brass gingerbread girl and gingerbread boy charms
Twelve 3/8-inch brass snowflake charms or sequins
Red and white acrylic craft paints and small paintbrush (optional)
Black permanent marker
Sharp craft scissors
Glue gun and glue sticks
Any size coordinating basket with straight sides

Finished Size: Assembled basket trim measures about 10 inches across x 4-1/2 inches high.

Directions:
CUTTING: Using black marker and following charts, draw outline of charts onto plastic canvas as directed. Cut out the shapes, leaving the bars along the outline of each.

STITCHING: Working with 18-in. to 20-in. lengths of yarn or floss, refer to charts and instructions to stitch pieces. See Fig. 1 for stitch illustrations.

Do not knot yarn or floss. Instead, leave a 1-in. tail on the back of the plastic canvas and work the next few stitches over it. To end a strand, run it under completed stitches of the same color and clip close to work.

House: Separate six-strand embroi-

dery floss and use the number of strands as directed.

Using Continental stitch and six strands of light brown floss, stitch the entire house.

Fill in door with 12 strands of white floss and straight stitch. Then overcast outside edges of door.

Place door right side up on right side of house as shown in photo. Use one strand of red metallic thread to straight-stitch stripes onto door, attaching door to house as you stitch.

Use 12 strands of white floss and

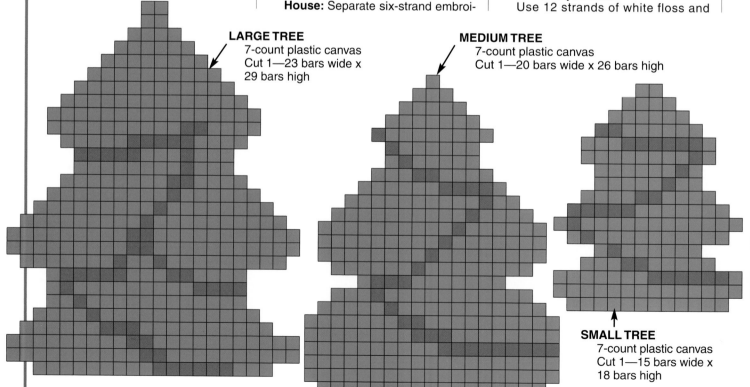

LARGE TREE
7-count plastic canvas
Cut 1—23 bars wide x 29 bars high

MEDIUM TREE
7-count plastic canvas
Cut 1—20 bars wide x 26 bars high

SMALL TREE
7-count plastic canvas
Cut 1—15 bars wide x 18 bars high

straight stitch to fill in each candy cane. Then overcast around outside edges.

Place the candy canes right sides up on the house as shown in the photo. Use a single strand of red metallic thread to add spiraling stripes to the candy canes, attaching them to the sides of the house as you stitch.

Use six strands of white rayon floss to straight-stitch the roof as shown on the chart. Add French knots to the bottom edge of the roof. Then overcast all of the outside edges.

Glue roof right side up to top edge of house.

Trees: Stitch trim on trees with dark green yarn and turkey loop stitch, leaving 1/4-in. loops. In same way, fill in trees with light green yarn and turkey loop stitch.

Drape gold thread across front of each tree for trim as shown in photo. Thread needle with green floss and hand-tack gold trim to trees as needed.

Referring to photo for placement, glue sequins or snowflake charms to right side of each tree as shown in photo.

FINISHING: Glue small tree to back of right edge of medium tree. Glue house centered between medium and large trees.

Paint mouth, buttons and bow tie on gingerbread charms red and zigzag trim white if desired. Let dry.

Glue gingerbread boy to large tree at left of house and gingerbread girl to medium tree at right as shown in photo.

Glue assembled basket trim to side of basket as shown in photo. ☆

DOOR
10-count plastic canvas
Cut 1—14 bars wide x 20 bars high

CANDY CANES
10-count plastic canvas
Cut 2—4 bars wide x 20 bars high

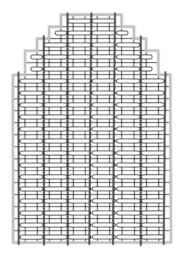

Fig. 1

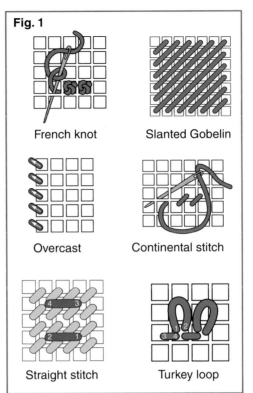

French knot

Slanted Gobelin

Overcast

Continental stitch

Straight stitch

Turkey loop

DECORATED BASKET COLOR KEY

CONTINENTAL STITCH
✎ Light brown floss
TURKEY LOOP
■ Dark green yarn
■ Light green yarn
FRENCH KNOT
● White rayon floss
OVERCAST
— Light brown floss
= White rayon floss
BACKSTITCH
— Red metallic thread
SLANTED GOBELIN
⁄ White rayon floss
STRAIGHT STITCH
— White rayon floss

HOUSE
14-count plastic canvas
Cut 1—41 bars wide x 46 bars high

ROOF
10-count plastic canvas
Cut 1—35 bars wide x 16 bars high

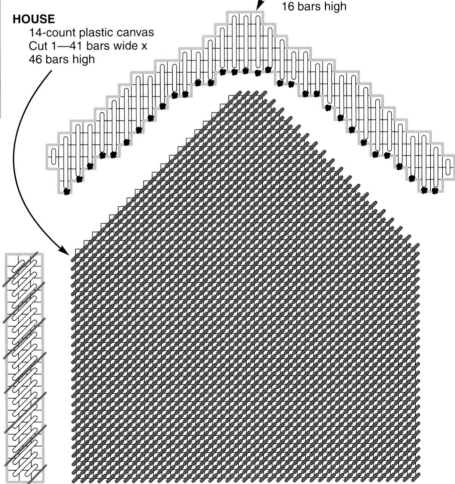

Festive Sweatshirt's Abloom with the Season

YOU will be carrying glad tidings when you wear this petal-perfect apparel!

To make her pretty applique, Cheryl Ricketts of Washington, Illinois first "wove" a basket from strips of tan bias tape, then layered country prints and plaids to create the poinsettias.

"It only looks complicated," assures Cheryl. "Beginners and experienced crafters alike will find the design's a delight from start to finish."

Materials Needed:
Patterns on next page
Tracing paper and pencil
Dark green sweatshirt
100% cotton or cotton-blend fabrics—
1/8 yard each or scraps of three different green plaid or checked fabrics for leaves; 1/8 yard each or scraps of four different small red prints or checks for flowers; and 1/8 yard or scrap of red and green plaid for background
One package of tan 1/2-inch-wide single-fold bias tape
1/2 yard of 5/8-inch-wide green, red and gold metallic striped ribbon
All-purpose thread—green, red and tan

1/4 yard of paper-backed fusible web
1/2 yard of tear-away stabilizer or typing paper
Twelve 6mm gold beads for centers of flowers
10-inch x 8-inch piece of corrugated cardboard
Standard sewing supplies

Finished Size: The basket applique measures 10 inches across x 10 inches high and is shown on an Adult size Large sweatshirt. The design can be enlarged or reduced on a copy machine to fit other size garments.

Directions:
Pre-wash fabrics without fabric softeners, washing colors separately. Dry and press fabrics. Wash and dry sweatshirt, following manufacturer's instructions.

WEAVING: Place cardboard on a flat work surface. Center a 7-in. x 5-in. piece of fusible web paper-side down on cardboard and pin edges to secure.

Cut five 7-in.-long pieces of tan bias tape and one 7-in.-long piece of ribbon for horizontal weaving strips. Place bias tape and ribbon right side up over fusible web as shown in Fig. 1a. Pin both ends of each to secure.

Cut nine 5-in.-long pieces of tan bias tape for vertical weaving strips. Weave strips one at a time through each crosswise strip.

When all strips are woven and intersect squarely as shown in Fig. 1b, remove pins and press strips lightly to hold them in place.

CUTTING: Trace basket pattern onto folded tracing paper. Cut out and open for a complete pattern.

Center basket pattern over right side of woven piece with grainline on pattern parallel to vertical strips. Trace around outside edge of pattern. Remove pattern and machine-stitch over traced line through strips and fusible web.

Cut out basket through all layers just outside stitched line. Press on paper side to fuse strips, following manufacturer's directions. Set basket aside.

Trace flower, leaf and background patterns as directed onto paper side of fusible web, leaving 1/2 in. between shapes. Cut shapes apart.

Fuse shapes to wrong side of fabrics as directed on patterns. Transfer inside design lines on three small flowers by straight-stitching on lines traced on paper backing. Cut shapes out along traced lines.

APPLIQUE: Remove paper backing from shapes and arrange them on the center front of sweatshirt, placing small flowers over large flowers and overlapping shapes as shown in photo. Fuse shapes in place.

Position tear-away stabilizer or typing paper on wrong side of garment behind applique area.

Using red thread and a medium satin stitch, applique around background.

Using tan thread and a wide satin stitch, applique around sides and bottom of basket.

Using green thread and a medium satin stitch, applique around the visible edges of each leaf.

Using red thread and a medium satin stitch, applique around the large flowers, the small flowers and over the inside design lines.

Remove stabilizer or typing paper. Pull loose threads to wrong side. Tie off and clip threads close to knots.

FINISHING: Hand-sew beads to centers of small flowers in groups of four.

Tie the remaining ribbon into a bow. Hand-stitch the bow to the basket where shown in photo.

Add to your festive wardrobe! ☆

Fig. 1a Weaving basket

Paper-backed fusible web

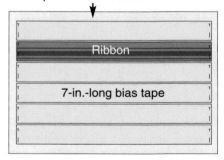

Fig. 1b Adding vertical strips

5-in.-long bias tape

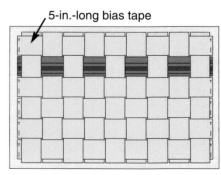

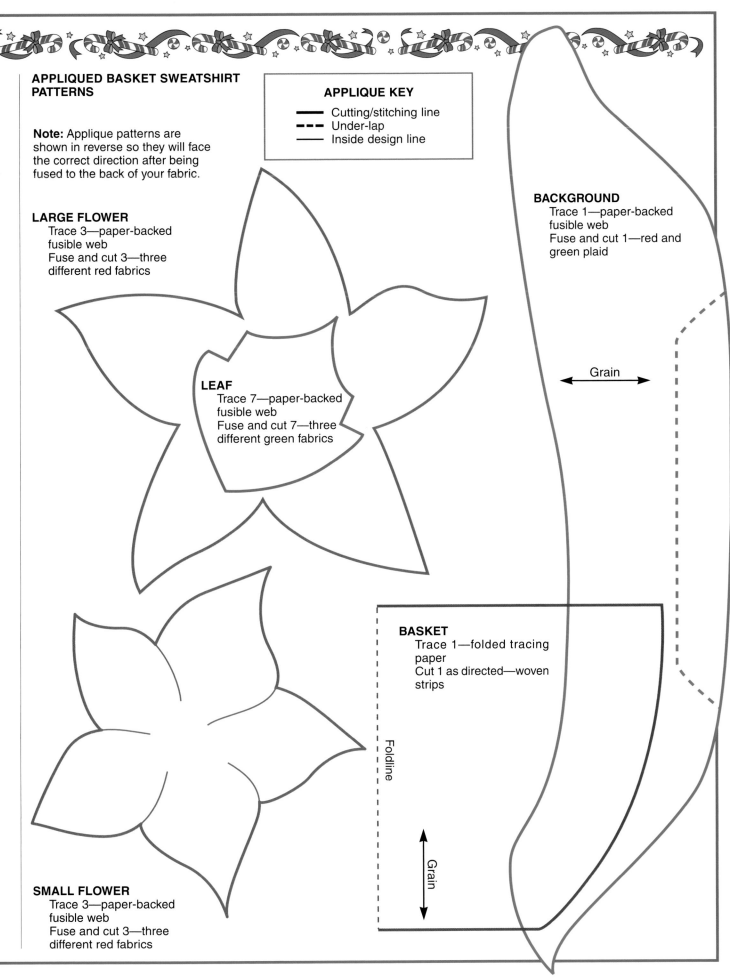

APPLIQUED BASKET SWEATSHIRT PATTERNS

Note: Applique patterns are shown in reverse so they will face the correct direction after being fused to the back of your fabric.

APPLIQUE KEY
— Cutting/stitching line
– – – Under-lap
— Inside design line

LARGE FLOWER
Trace 3—paper-backed fusible web
Fuse and cut 3—three different red fabrics

LEAF
Trace 7—paper-backed fusible web
Fuse and cut 7—three different green fabrics

BACKGROUND
Trace 1—paper-backed fusible web
Fuse and cut 1—red and green plaid

Grain

BASKET
Trace 1—folded tracing paper
Cut 1 as directed—woven strips

Foldline

Grain

SMALL FLOWER
Trace 3—paper-backed fusible web
Fuse and cut 3—three different red fabrics

Magnets Are Merry Notable

KEEPING TRACK of your family's Christmas wish lists is a sweet task with these plastic canvas magnets. The lively pair attracts smiles aplenty from all ages, reveals crafter Mary Cosgrove of Rockville, Connecticut.

She shares instructions here for her Santa memo holder and candy cane pen keeper. "You can finish them in a flash," she points out, "then move on to other holiday activities."

Materials Needed:
Charts on this page and the next page
One sheet of 7-count clear plastic canvas
Worsted-weight or plastic canvas yarn—
  1 yard of black, 3 yards of green,
  2 yards of pink, 7 yards of red,
  8 yards of white and 7 yards of yellow
3 yards of red metallic cord
5 inches of 1/2-inch-wide self-adhesive
  magnetic strip
Size 16 tapestry needle
Black permanent marker
Sharp craft scissors
3-inch-wide x 4-1/2-inch-
  long pad of paper
Pen

Finished Size: Santa memo holder measures 6-1/2 inches across x 6-1/4 inches tall. Candy cane pen holder is about 3 inches wide x 6 inches tall.

Directions:
CUTTING: Using black marker and following charts, draw outline of charts onto plastic canvas as directed.

Cut out shapes, leaving the bars along the outline on each.

STITCHING: Working with 18-in. to 20-in. lengths of yarn, follow charts and individual instructions to stitch each piece. See Fig. 1 on opposite page for stitch illustrations.

Do not knot yarn on back of work. Instead, leave a 1-in. tail on the back of the plastic canvas and work the next few stitches over it. To end a strand, run yarn on back of canvas under completed stitches of the same color and clip yarn close to work.

Santa's list: Using Continental stitch and yarn, stitch face pink, eyes black, hat, nose and mouth red and beard and fur trim on hat white. Stitch top edge of Santa's list green and background of Santa's list yellow as shown on chart.

Add black backstitching around eyes over Continental stitches. Add green straight stitching for lettering over Continental stitches.

Overcast edges of cutout with yellow, edges of list with green, Santa's beard with white and Santa's hat with red.

Cut a 3-in.-long piece of magnetic strip. Adhere strip to back of Santa.

Slip the paper pad into opening as shown in photo.

Candy cane pen holder: Use slanted Gobelin stitch and red and white yarns to stitch candy cane and holder, leaving edges unstitched. Overcast top and bottom edges of holder with matching yarns.

Place holder right side up on right side of candy cane with unstitched edges positioned as shown in photo. Use red metallic cord to whipstitch holder to one side of candy cane. Then overcast around candy cane to other side.

Whipstitch remaining edge of holder to candy cane and continue to overcast around to starting point.

Cut remaining piece of magnetic strip in half crosswise. Glue strips onto top and bottom of back of candy cane.

Insert pen into holder. Place both pieces on your refrigerator. ☆

SANTA'S LIST
43 bars x 41 bars
Cut 1—plastic canvas
Remove shaded section

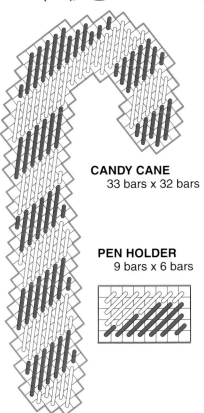

CANDY CANE
33 bars x 32 bars

PEN HOLDER
9 bars x 6 bars

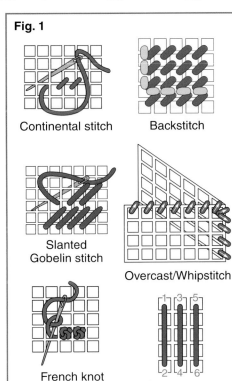

Fig. 1

Continental stitch

Backstitch

Slanted Gobelin stitch

Overcast/Whipstitch

French knot

Straight stitch

SANTA'S LIST AND CANDY CANE HOLDER COLOR KEY

CONTINENTAL STITCH
- Black
- Green
- Pink
- Red
- White
- Yellow

FRENCH KNOT
- Green

SLANTED GOBELIN STITCH
- Red
- White

BACKSTITCH
- Black
- Green

STRAIGHT STITCH
- Green

OVERCAST/WHIPSTITCH
- Green
- Red
- Red metallic
- White
- Yellow

Her Jewelry Will Jingle All the Way

IN TUNE with the season is this colorful crocheted necklace stitched by Joyce Colpetzer from Lake City, Tennessee. She added an edging of jingle bells and beads as she made her rounds.

"You could substitute colorful buttons for the beads and bells," Joyce suggests. "Either way, the necklace makes a festive accent."

Materials Needed:
Size 10 red crochet cotton—approximately 200 yards
Steel crochet hooks—size 7 (1.5mm) and 10 (.75mm)
Thirty-one 10mm gold jingle bells
10mm wooden beads—10 each of green, red and white
3/8-inch button
Large-eye hand-sewing needle

Finished Size: Necklace is about 28 inches long.

Directions:
Wind about 12 yards of crochet thread into a ball.

Row 1: Using size 7 crochet hook and thread from wound ball and from original ball held together as one, ch 204, work 1 sc in seventh ch from hk, sc in each of next chs across: 198 scs. Fasten off.

Row 2: Using size 10 crochet hook, attach thread from original ball with a sc 40 sts from end opposite loop. * Ch 5, sk one sc, work 1 sc in next sc; repeat from * until there are 62 ch-5 spaces centered along Row 1. Fasten off.

Row 3: String bells and beads onto thread from original ball in the following sequence: Bell, green bead, bell, white bead, bell, red bead. String remaining bells and beads in the same order, ending with a bell. Then attach thread to first sc of Row 2, sl st to center of first ch-5 sp, * ch 3, slide next bell or bead close to hk, ch 1 loosely so bell or bead can dangle from ch worked, ch 3, sc in next ch-5 sp; repeat from * across, adding remaining bells and beads; sl st across last ch-5 sp to last sc. Fasten off.

Weave in loose ends and hand-sew button to end of necklace opposite loop.

Accent a favorite top with your festive holiday jewelry! ☆

ABBREVIATIONS

ch(s)	chain(s)
hk	hook
sc(s)	single crochet(s)
sl st	slip stitch
sk	skip
st(s)	stitch(es)
*	Instructions following asterisk are repeated as instructed.

Creche Sets a Spirited Scene

PIECING TOGETHER the true meaning of the season is what this simple Nativity—which is also a child's puzzle—is designed to do.

"The easy-to-cut pieces are sized just right for small hands to help assemble," details Debbie Gauthier of Kapuskasing, Ontario, who shares the pattern below. "And whether you display it on a coffee table, windowsill or under the tree, it's a wonderful reminder of what Christmas is all about."

Materials Needed:
Patterns on this page
Tracing paper and pencil
Stylus or dry ballpoint pen
6-inch square of 3/4-inch-thick pine
Scroll or band saw
Sandpaper and tack cloth
Light brown stain and soft cloth
Palette or paper plate
*Acrylic craft paints—flesh, green,
    gold and red*
Small flat paintbrush

Finished Size: Wood Nativity measures 5 inches across x 5-1/4 inches high.

Directions:
Trace the patterns onto a piece of tracing paper. Turn tracing paper pattern over and rub flat side of pencil lead over traced lines to darken.

Place pattern right side up over wood. Trace over pattern lines with stylus or dry ballpoint pen to transfer cutting lines of pattern onto the wood.

Carefully cut out wood pieces with scroll or band saw, following cutting lines on pattern. Pieces cut from the wooden square are the figures used in the Nativity scene.

Sand each piece smooth and wipe with tack cloth to remove sanding dust.

Apply stain to all sides of all pieces with soft cloth. Let dry.

Place small amounts of paints on paper plate or palette as needed. Paint both sides of pieces as directed at right, extending paints onto sides of each. Apply a second coat as needed for complete coverage, allowing drying time between coats.

Paint star gold. With flesh, paint

baby and faces and hands on Mary and Joseph as shown on pattern. When dry, paint green and red garments. Let dry.

Position star and figures as shown in photo above.

Place on the mantel or by the tree... and watch for happy reactions! ☆

WOOD NATIVITY PATTERN
Trace 1—tracing paper
Cut 1 as directed—3/4-in. pine

—— Cutting line
—— Painting line

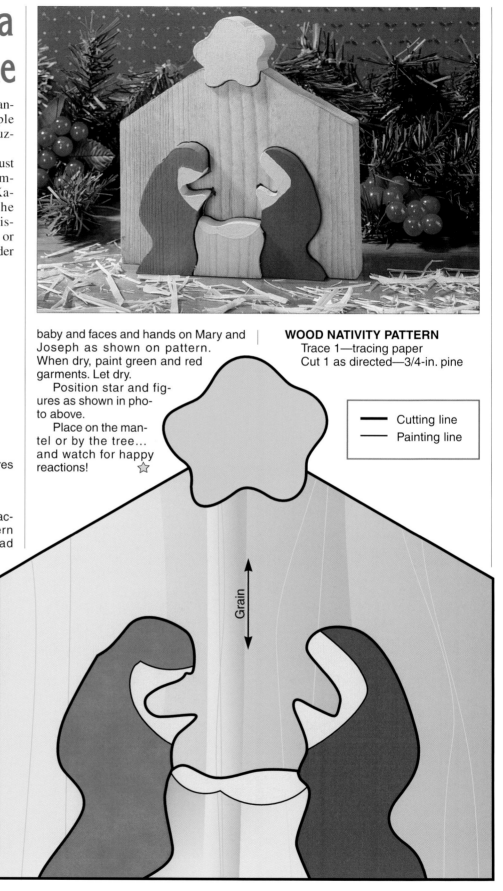

Tree Trim Is Country at Heart

PINING for a way to add a touch of yesteryear to your evergreen? It's sew easy—with this patchwork accent from Chris Pfefferkorn of New Braunfels, Texas.

Old-fashioned crazy quilting lends a nostalgic look to the ornament, which can also double as a pin cushion, package topper or necklace.

Materials Needed:
Pattern below
Tracing paper and pencil
Small scraps of print or solid silk, taffeta, faille, satin or velvet fabrics in colors of choice
Matching all-purpose thread
12 inches of gold metallic rickrack
32 inches of gold cording
White six-strand embroidery floss
Polyester stuffing
Standard sewing supplies

Finished Size: Heart measures 3-1/4 inches high x 4-1/4 inches across without hanger.

Directions:
Cut two 6-in. squares of fabric, one for the backing of the heart and one for the base of crazy quilting.

Trace heart pattern onto tracing paper. Place the pattern on the right side of one 6-in. square of fabric. Using a straight stitch, sew over traced outline of heart. Remove pattern.

To crazy quilt, pin a scrap of fabric right side up to center of stitched heart shape. Place different scrap of fabric on top with right sides together and one edge matching as shown in Fig. 1a. Sew matching edges together with a 1/4-in. seam, sewing through both fabrics and heart base. Turn top piece up and press along seam line. Pin this piece to heart base.

Add a third fabric scrap as shown in Fig. 1b. Trim excess fabric from seam as needed and turn scrap right side up. Press along seam line and pin this piece to heart base as shown in Fig. 1c.

Continue to crazy quilt in this way until heart base is covered and fabric scraps extend at least 1/4 in. beyond stitched outline of heart base.

Separate six-strand floss and use two strands to feather-stitch over seam lines as shown in photo. See Fig. 2 for stitch illustration.

Trim around outside of heart 1/4 in. outside stitched outline.

Starting at top center of heart, pin rickrack to right side around stitched heart shape and overlap ends at starting point. Sew rickrack in place, stitching down the center of the rickrack and making sure stitching is just inside stitched outline of heart.

Place completed heart over backing fabric with right sides together. Straight-stitch around the outside edge just inside the stitching lines, leaving an opening for turning.

Trim point and clip center top to stitching. Turn right side out through opening. Stuff the heart firmly. Turn the raw edges of the opening in and stitch the opening closed.

Fold gold cord in half. Hand-stitch center of cord to center top of heart. Knot ends of cord to prevent raveling and trim cord close to knots. Tie ends of cord in a large bow as shown in photo.

Hang from a tree branch. ☆

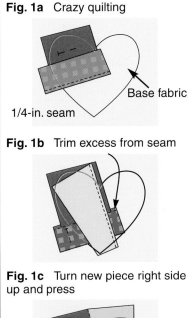

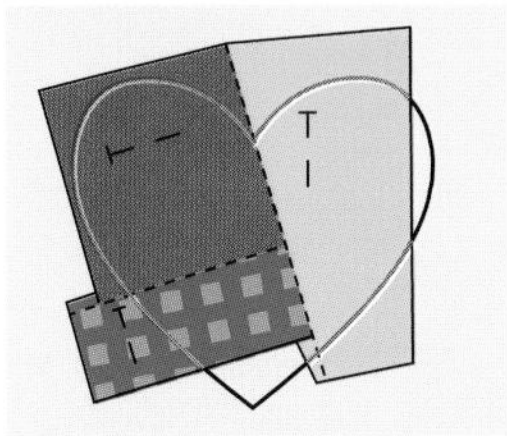

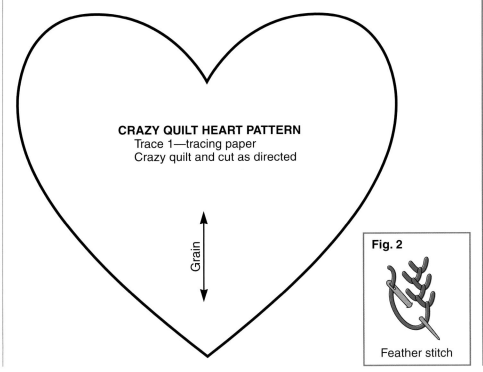

CRAZY QUILT HEART PATTERN
Trace 1—tracing paper
Crazy quilt and cut as directed

Grain

Fig. 2

Feather stitch

Fig. 1a Crazy quilting

Base fabric

1/4-in. seam

Fig. 1b Trim excess from seam

Fig. 1c Turn new piece right side up and press

81

Thread a 24-in.-long piece of ribbon onto needle. Place two card sections with wrong sides together and edges matching. Starting at the bottom, stitch the two card sections together, sewing through first hole and leaving a 2-in. tail of ribbon.

Continue to whipstitch along edge, stitching through each hole twice to the top. See Fig. 1 for stitch illustration. Leave tail of ribbon to curl later.

In the same way, add another card section to opposite edge of first card section. Repeat, adding remaining sections to unstitched edges. Then whipstitch unstitched edges of first and last sections together.

Gently fold each section in half lengthwise with right sides together to make tree shape as shown in photo.

Stitch remaining lengths of ribbon through any three holes at top of tree and tie a knot in center of each. Curl ends with scissors. Trim as desired. Glue pom-pom to top of tree.

"Plant" a grove of trees on a coffee table or windowsill.   ☆

CARD TREE PATTERN

Trace 1—tracing paper
Cut 4—used Christmas cards
X = punched holes

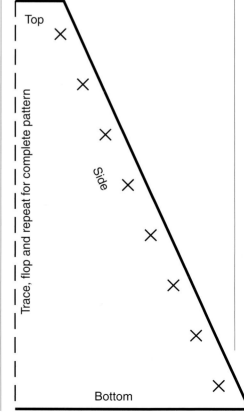

Evergreens Sprout from Cards

NOTING how many holiday greeting cards she had on hand, an idea took root in Adriana Rensink's mind. "I couldn't just throw them away," the Glendale, California crafter tells.

Instead, she used the cards to create a forest of festive firs to top tables in her home. The project is a fun one for youngsters to try with a little help from a grown-up, Adriana advises.

Materials Needed (for each):

Pattern on this page
Tracing paper, pencil and scissors
Four Christmas cards that are at least 4-1/2 inches square
1/4-inch round paper punch
3-2/3 yards of curling ribbon in color of choice
Yarn needle
5/8-inch pom-pom in color of choice
White (tacky) glue

Finished Size: The card trees pictured each measure about 5 inches tall x 5 inches across.

Directions:

Trace pattern onto tracing paper as directed. Cut out shape on outside traced lines.

Place pattern on front of card, positioning it over design area of card you want to use. Trace around pattern. Repeat on three more cards. Cut out on traced lines.

Use paper punch to make holes at each X along sides of each section.

Cut ribbon into four 24-in. lengths and three 12-in. lengths.

Fig. 1

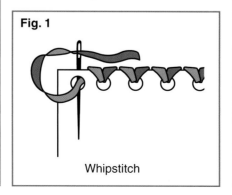

Whipstitch

Edging Round: Ch 1, sc in ends of Rows 32-11; work 1 hdc in ends of Rows 10-1; working in beginning chs, hdc in each of first seven chs, sc in each of next six chs, hdc in each of last 11 chs; work 2 hdcs in end of Row 1; dc in ends of Rows 2-11; hdc in end of Row 12, work 2 scs in first unworked st of Row 12, sc in each of next seven unworked sts of Row 12; sc in ends of Rows 13-31; work 2 scs in end of Row 32, sc in each st across row to last st of Row 32, work 2 scs in last st; sl st in first sc of round. Fasten off.

Joining Round: Holding both completed stockings together with edges matching, join red yarn with sc in first st of edging round; join stockings by working 1 sc in each st around to top of stocking; working in front piece of stocking only, sc in each of next 18 sts, sl st in first sc of edging round; ch 6, sl st in first ch for hanging loop; working in back piece of stocking only, sc in each st across back; sl st in st joining front and back. Fasten off and weave in loose ends.

Attach velvet bow to top as shown in photo if desired.

SMALL STOCKING (make two): With variegated yarn, ch 13.

Row 1: Sc in second ch from hk and in each of the next chs across: 12 scs.

Rows 2-6: Ch 1, turn, sc in each st across: 12 scs.

Row 7: Ch 1, turn, sc in each of next eight scs, leaving last four sts unworked: 8 scs.

Rows 8-16: Ch 1, turn, sc in each sc across: 8 scs.

Edging Round: Ch 1, sc in ends of Rows 16-6; hdc in ends of Rows 5-1; working in beginning chs, hdc in each of first four chs, sc in each of next three chs, hdc in each of last five chs; work 2 hdcs in end of Row 1; dc in ends of Rows 2-5; hdc in end of Row 6, work 2 scs in first unworked st of Row 6, sc in each of next three unworked sts; sc in ends of Rows 7-16; work 2 scs in first st of Row 16, sc across row to last st, work 2 scs in last st of Row 16; sl st in first sc of round. Fasten off.

Joining Round: Holding both completed stockings together with edges matching, join green yarn with sc in first st of edging round; join stockings by working 1 sc in each st around to top of stocking; working in front piece of stocking only, sc in each of next 10 sts; sl st in first sc of edging round; ch 6, sl st in first ch for hanging loop; working in back piece of stocking only, sc in each st across back; sl st in st joining front and back. Fasten off and weave in loose ends.

Pack stockings full of goodies! ☆

Large or Small, Stockings Are a Sure Fit for Christmas!

SIZED to suit any holiday occasion, these colorfully crocheted stockings are fleet feats indeed!

Crafter Connie Folse of Thibodaux, Louisiana stitched the smaller one to be used as a table favor or tree ornament. The larger sock is ideal for stocking with candies and other goodies and hanging on the mantel.

Materials Needed (for one large and one small stocking):

4-ply worsted-weight yarn—1 ounce each of red and green and 3 ounces of green, red and white variegated
Size G (4.25mm) crochet hook or size hook needed to obtain the correct gauge
Tapestry needle
Purchased 4-inch red velvet bow (optional)
Scissors

Gauge: Working in sc, 7 sts and 7 rows = 2 inches.

Finished Size: Large stocking is 10-1/4 inches long x 9 inches wide. Small stocking is 6 inches long x 5 inches wide.

Directions:

LARGE STOCKING (make two): With variegated yarn, ch 25.

Row 1: Sc in second ch from hk and in each of the next chs across: 24 scs.

Rows 2-12: Ch 1, turn, sc in each sc across: 24 scs.

Row 13: Ch 1, turn, sc in each of next 16 scs, leaving last eight sts unworked: 16 scs.

Rows 14-32: Ch 1, turn, sc in each sc across: 16 scs.

ABBREVIATIONS

ch(s)	chain(s)
dc(s)	double crochet(s)
hdc(s)	half double crochet(s)
lp(s)	loop(s)
sc(s)	single crochet(s)
sl st	slip stitch

Heirloom Album Has Memories Well Covered

A STITCH IN TIME—that is exactly what you'll have when you collect precious Christmas keepsakes inside this pretty portfolio from Betty Souther of Dos Palos, California.

The plastic canvas cover wraps around any standard-size binder. "I created the needlepoint design to give it a classic look," details Betty. "Everything from photos to drawings, cards and more can be stored in here."

Materials Needed:
Charts on next page
One standard 1-1/2-inch
   three-ring binder
Two 13-1/2-inch x 22-1/2-inch sheets
   of clear 7-count plastic canvas
Worsted-weight yarn—100 yards of
   dark green, 25 yards of light green,
   4 yards of medium green, 2 yards
   of pink, 25 yards of red and 52
   yards of white
Size 16 tapestry needle
Sharp craft scissors

Finished Size: Photo album cover is 24 inches wide x 12 inches high when opened.

Directions:
CUTTING: Remembering to count bars and not holes, cut two 80-bar x 71-bar pieces for front and back of cover and one 80-bar x 19-bar piece for the spine. Also cut two 80-bar x 16-bar pieces for inside flaps. The inside flaps are not stitched.

STITCHING: Working with 18-in. to 20-in. lengths of yarn, follow charts and instructions that follow to stitch pieces. See Fig. 1 for stitch illustrations.

Do not knot yarn on back of work. Instead, leave a 1-in. tail on the back of the plastic canvas and work the next few stitches over it. To end a strand, run yarn under completed stitches of the same color on back of canvas and clip yarn close to work.

Front: Use red Continental stitches to add inside and outside borders and frame to create four panels as shown on chart.

Use dark green Continental stitches to complete each letter inside panels as shown on chart. Complete design in each panel with Continental stitch and medium green, red and pink as shown on charts. Use white Continental stitches to fill in background of each panel.

Use light green Continental stitches to stitch middle of inside border. Then use light green slanted Gobelin and Continental stitches to fill in between red inside and outside borders.

Use red, light green and dark green Continental stitches to complete patterned border, leaving edges unstitched.

Back: Fill in back with dark green Continental stitches, leaving edges unstitched.

Spine: Use dark green Continental stitches to add inside border.

Add lettering with red Continental stitches. Then fill in background inside border with white Continental stitches.

Use white Scotch and Continental stitches to stitch around bordered lettering, leaving outside edges unstitched.

ASSEMBLY: Place the completed pieces right side up on a flat surface, placing back on the left, the spine in the center and the front on the right.

Using dark green, whipstitch one long edge of spine to matching edge of back. Overcast short edge of spine and then whipstitch matching edge of front to remaining long edge of spine. Overcast along remaining short edge of spine and then continue along edge of back, stopping 17 bars from end.

Position inside flap on wrong side of cover with edges matching. Whipstitch inside flap to cover. Then continue to overcast edge of cover, stopping 17 bars from front. Position inside flap on inside of front as for back and whipstitch inside flap in place.

Continue to overcast edge of front to starting point.

Fold binder covers back and insert binder into the flaps on the inside of stitched cover.

Fill with festive family mementos and enjoy for years to come. ☆

PHOTO ALBUM COLOR KEY
CONTINENTAL STITCH
🖊 Dark green
🖊 Light green
🖊 Medium green
🖊 Pink
🖊 Red
🖊 White
SLANTED GOEBLIN
🖊 Light green
SCOTCH STITCH
🖊 White
OVERCAST/WHIPSTITCH
— Dark green

Fig. 1

Continental stitch

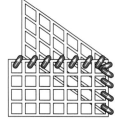

Overcast/Whipstitch

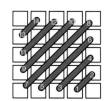

Scotch stitch

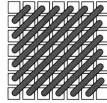

Slanted
Gobelin stitch

PHOTO ALBUM CHARTS

FRONT
80 bars x 71 bars

SPINE
80 bars x 19 bars

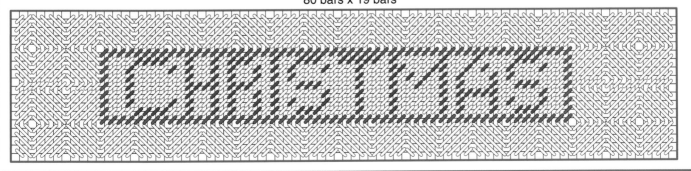

Charming Gift Trims Are Sure To Grow on You

TOP presents with these poinsettia and holly trims and you'll see smiles crop up well before any wrapping paper's been removed!

Designer Darlene Polachic of Saskatoon, Saskatchewan regularly makes the pretty package tie-ons for her clan from leftover scraps of felt.

Materials Needed (for both):
Patterns on this page
Tracing paper and pencil
Felt—9-inch square of red,
8-inch square of green and 1-inch
square of yellow
White all-purpose thread
Gold metallic seed beads for center
of poinsettia and holly berries
Gold metallic thread
Standard sewing supplies

Finished Size: Poinsettia measures 4 inches across. Holly gift trim measures 4-3/4 inches across x 3 inches high.

Directions:
Trace patterns onto tracing paper. Cut shapes from felt as directed on patterns.

POINSETTIA: Stack two poinsettia leaf shapes with edges matching. Sew the two shapes together with a straight stitch, stitching where shown on pattern. Sew two remaining leaf shapes together in same way.

Stack two poinsettia flower shapes on top of each other with edges matching. Pin to hold.

Pin the two completed leaves to the back of the flower as shown in photo. Sew the layers together with a straight stitch, sewing where indicated on the pattern and catching the leaf shapes in the stitching as you sew.

Center and pin the yellow flower center on top of the stitched pieces. Straight-

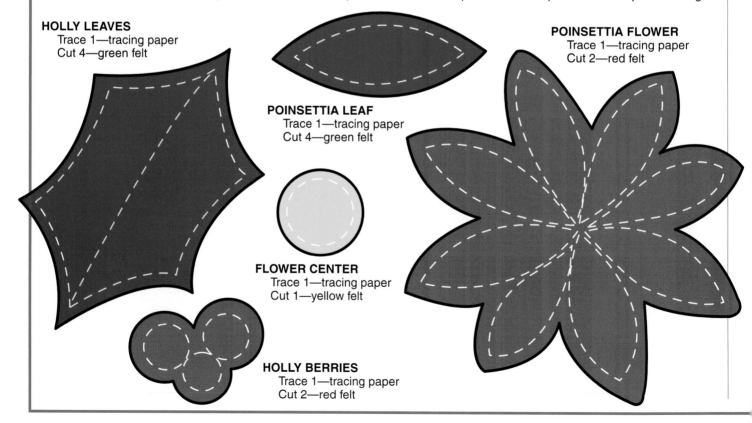

HOLLY LEAVES
Trace 1—tracing paper
Cut 4—green felt

POINSETTIA LEAF
Trace 1—tracing paper
Cut 4—green felt

FLOWER CENTER
Trace 1—tracing paper
Cut 1—yellow felt

HOLLY BERRIES
Trace 1—tracing paper
Cut 2—red felt

POINSETTIA FLOWER
Trace 1—tracing paper
Cut 2—red felt

stitch around the flower center where shown on pattern.

Hand-sew gold seed beads evenly around edge of flower center and sew several in a group in the center.

Pull all threads to back and fasten off.

Stitch a piece of gold metallic thread through one petal of flower, leaving ends loose to tie trim to gift.

HOLLY: Stack two holly leaf shapes with edges matching. Sew the leaves together, stitching where shown on pattern. Sew the two remaining holly leaves together in same way.

Pin leaves side by side with two end points meeting.

Stack the holly berry shapes with edges matching. Place the berries over the points of the holly leaves as shown in the photo. Sew around the three berries where shown on the pattern, catching the points of the holly leaves in the stitching.

Hand-sew a seed bead to center of each berry.

Pull all threads to back and fasten off.

Stitch a piece of gold metallic thread through one berry, leaving ends loose to tie tag to gift.

Attach trims to your gifts! ☆

Evergreen Neckwear Ties Up Yuletide in Fine Style

HELP Dad branch out a bit during December by bundling up this handsome Christmas tree tie for him to wear! It's sure to make a festive statement at any kind of gathering.

Verlyn King of Tremonton, Utah turned to a common quilting pattern called prairie point to make the pine design. Aside from ties, you can brighten up a winter scarf or fingertip towels with the motif as well.

Materials Needed:
3/4-inch-high x 1/8-inch-thick wooden star
Tie tack and back (found in jewelry section of most craft stores)
White (tacky) glue
Gold metallic craft paint
Small flat paintbrush
Purchased necktie—red solid
44-inch-wide fabrics—1/8 yard each or scraps of dark green and white polka dot, small dark green and white check and brown solid
Matching all-purpose thread
Hand-sewing needle
Straight pins
Pinking shears
Straight scissors
Ruler
Quilter's marking pen or pencil

Finished Size: Design area of tree is about 3 inches wide x 5-3/4 inches long.

Directions:
STAR TIE TACK: Apply glue to center of one side of wooden star. Press flat side of base of tie tack pin into glue, squeezing glue up around edges of base. Let dry.

Paint all sides of star gold. Let dry.

TREE: Draw a 3-1/8-in. square, a 2-1/2-in. square and a 2-in. square on wrong side of dark green and white pol-

ka dot fabric. Repeat on wrong side of small dark green and white check fabric. Cut out six squares with pinking shears for branches of tree.

Draw a 1-1/2-in. square on the wrong side of the brown solid for the tree trunk. Cut out the square with straight scissors.

Fold and press 1/4 in. along one edge of brown fabric square to the wrong side. Fold and press opposite raw edges to center on wrong side to make a 1-1/4-in. tall x 3/4-in.-wide tree trunk.

For branches, fold and press each remaining square in half diagonally with wrong sides together. Then fold and press each in half diagonally again, making six triangles. Pin each triangle to hold.

Center bottom edge of tree trunk 1 in. above point of tie. Pin to hold.

Center and pin largest dark green and white check triangle with pinked edge down over top raw edge of tree trunk, leaving about 1 in. of trunk exposed as shown in photo.

Center and pin the largest dark green and white polka dot triangle over the first, leaving about 3/4 in. of the triangle exposed.

Pin medium and then small triangles to tie in same order, leaving about 3/4 in. of each exposed.

Thread hand-sewing needle with brown thread and hand-applique outside edges of trunk to tie. See Fig. 1 for stitch illustration.

Thread hand-sewing needle with

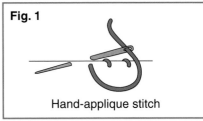

Fig. 1

Hand-applique stitch

green thread and hand-applique exposed edges of branches to tie.

Attach tie tack to top of tree .

Give to Dad or Grandpa to wear for a family get-together! ☆

Tree Topper Stirs Up Heartfelt Sentiment!

RISING right to the top, this angel tree topper is sure to mix plenty of meaning into your holiday decor. To create the spirited figure, Julie Miller relied on a secret ingredient—a common wooden kitchen spoon!

"The bowl of the spoon serves as the angel's face and the handle forms her body," the Plummer, Idaho crafter explains. "She's pretty sweet!"

Materials Needed:
Patterns on next page
Tracing paper and pencil
1/8 yard of paper-backed fusible web
10-inch-long wooden spoon
Empty cardboard tissue paper tube
1/2 yard of 44-inch-wide muslin
16-inch square of quilt batting
Fabric scraps—two 9-inch squares of red print for wings and scraps of several different red and green prints for appliques
3-inch x 6-inch piece of red felt
Matching all-purpose thread
10 yards of yellow acrylic yarn for hair
12-inch length of 1/4-inch wood dowel
12 inches of 1/4-inch-wide red satin ribbon
Powdered blush
Cotton swab
Two 3/8-inch gold jingle bells
2 inches of 1-inch-wide off-white lace
Two 1/3-inch-diameter wooden beads
Fine-line permanent markers—black and red
Craft wire
Wire cutters
Glue gun and glue sticks

3mm string pearls—6 inches each of gold and silver
Standard sewing supplies

Finished Size: The angel tree topper measures about 7-1/4 inches across x 11-1/2 inches tall.

Directions:
FACE: Use black and red markers to draw face onto rounded side of wooden spoon as shown in Fig. 1.

Place a small amount of powdered blush onto cotton swab and add to cheek area, using a circular motion.

BODY: Glue handle of wooden spoon to one side of inside of cardboard tube. Make sure bottom end of cardboard tube is even with end of spoon.

Cut a 6-in. x 16-in. piece of batting. Hand-sew a running stitch along one long edge of batting. See Fig. 2 for stitch illustration.

Draw up thread to gather slightly. Wrap gathered edge of batting around handle at base of bowl of spoon. Draw up thread around spoon and fasten off.

DRESS: Trace heart applique patterns onto paper side of fusible web as directed on patterns, leaving 1/2 in. between shapes. Cut shapes apart.

Fuse hearts onto wrong side of green print and red print fabrics, following manufacturer's directions. Cut out hearts on traced lines.

Cut two 3-in. squares of fusible web and fuse one to wrong side of green print and the other to wrong side of red print for patches. Cut one square into four smaller squares and the other into small rectangles.

Tear an 8-in. x 20-in. piece from muslin fabric for dress. Press one long edge 1/4 in. to the wrong side for the neck edge of dress.

Remove paper backing from hearts, squares and rectangles. Place shapes randomly on right side of the dress and fuse into place.

Use black marker to draw a broken line about 1/8 in. inside edges of the shapes for "stitches".

Sew short edges of dress together with right sides together and a 1/4-in. seam. Press seam open.

Hand-stitch along neck edge with running stitch, leaving thread attached. Slip dress over spoon with seam in back. Draw up thread to gather neck edge just below bowl of spoon, covering batting. Fasten off.

Glue lace around neck edge, overlapping ends in back.

ARMS: Tear a 12-in. square from muslin for arms. Fold opposite raw edges into center. Fold opposite long edges into center again, creating a long strip. Then fold strip in half lengthwise.

Pinch strip together at center. Tie center with thread to hold and glue center to back of neck.

Tie a piece of thread about 3/4 in. from each end of strip for hands.

HAIR: Wrap yellow yarn around 1/4-in. wood dowel. Wet yarn with water and blot to remove excess. Place yarn-wrapped dowel on cookie sheet and bake in oven at 225° until yarn is dry (about 45 minutes). Remove from oven and let cool.

Cut curled yarn into short ringlets. Glue yarn to the spoon as shown in the photo, starting at bottom of back of head and working to top of head. Trim yarn to desired length.

HEART WINGS: Trace the wing pattern onto the tracing paper as directed on the pattern.

Place a 9-in. square of batting on a flat surface. Center the 9-in. squares of red print fabric with right sides together on top of batting. Pin heart wing pattern on top with grainlines matching.

Sew all layers together, stitching on traced pattern lines and leaving an opening for turning. Remove pattern. Trim 1/4 in. outside stitching. Trim point and clip to stitching at top center of heart.

Turn right side out through opening with batting sandwiched between fab-

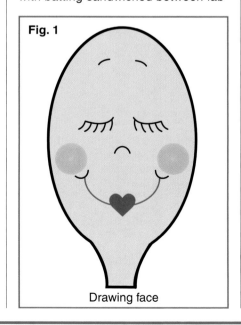

Fig. 1

Drawing face

rics. Turn raw edges of opening in. Hand-sew opening closed.

Machine-stitch around wings 1 in. from outside edge.

Glue wings centered to back of dress.

FELT HEART: Trace felt heart pattern onto tracing paper and cut out. Cut two hearts from red felt.

Place hearts together with edges matching, adding a bit of batting between the layers.

Hand-sew around hearts 1/8 in. from outside edges with matching thread and running stitch.

FINISHING: Glue a wooden bead to

opening of each arm for hands. Then glue felt heart between hands as shown in photo.

Twist gold and silver string beads together. Bring ends together to make a circle for halo. Glue halo to top of head.

Cut red ribbon in half and tie each half into a small bow. Glue a bow to back of halo and one to angel's neck. Glue a jingle bell to center of each bow.

Perch your angel on top of the Christmas tree! ☆

ANGEL TREE TOPPER PATTERNS

HEART APPLIQUES
Trace 3 each—paper-backed fusible web
Cut 3 each—fused green print or fused red print fabrics

FELT HEART
Trace 1— tracing paper
Cut 2—red felt

Grain

Fig. 2

Running stitch

HEART WINGS
Trace 1—tracing paper
Cut as directed

Trace, flop and repeat for complete pattern

Festive Frill Brightens Boughs

YOU'RE SURE to take a shine to this enlightening design for a tree trim! Not only can you finish it in a flash, but Lisa Reese of Greenwood, Indiana reveals that you'll likely have most of the materials on hand to make it.

Whether you hang it on a tree, wreath or garland, or dangle it in your kitchen window, it's certain to give a lovely lacy look to your holiday decor.

Materials Needed:
One 6-inch-round off-white crocheted doily
Sprigs of artificial wired pine bough
Baby's breath
Two small pinecones
3-inch x 1/4-inch red taper candle (for decorative use only)

Commercial fabric stiffener
1 yard of 1/4-inch-wide red satin ribbon
6 inches of 1/8-inch-wide off-white satin ribbon
Pearl florist spray (optional)
Glue gun and glue sticks

Finished Size: Candle ornament measures about 6 inches across.

Directions:
Apply fabric stiffener to doily, following manufacturer's directions. When dry, spray doily with pearl florist spray if desired. Let dry.

Glue pine sprigs, pinecones and baby's breath to the front of the doily, fanning them out from the bottom center as shown in photo.

Glue candle centered on greens.

Tie red ribbon into a small multi-loop bow. Trim ends as desired and glue bow to base of candle.

Thread off-white ribbon through center top of doily and tie ends in overhand knot for hanger.

Trim your tree...or hang this noel notion on a wreath! ☆

Homespun Lollipops Will Sweeten the Season

THESE dandy fabric "candies" will sugarcoat your spruce oh-so-tastefully this Christmas…and stick around to do it again for years to come!

Crafter Sandy McKenzie of Braham, Minnesota concocted her lollipops from leftover fabrics, Styrofoam balls and other simple supplies. "I like to hang them from the knobs on my kitchen cupboards, in addition to decorating the tree with them," she reveals.

Materials Needed (for each):
1-1/4-inch-diameter Styrofoam ball
Lollipop stick*
6-inch circle of Christmas print fabric
7 inches of green, red or white 1/8-
*   inch-wide satin ribbon or yarn*
6 inches of 1/8-inch-wide gold
*   metallic ribbon*
White (tacky) glue

* You can find lollipop sticks with the can-

dy making supplies at most craft stores. Or you can paint a 4-1/2-inch length of 1/8-inch-diameter wooden dowel white.

Finished Size: Each trim measures about 1-1/4 inches across x 5 inches long without hanger.

Directions:
Gently push the lollipop stick into Styrofoam ball, leaving about 3-1/2 in. of stick exposed. Remove stick and add glue to hole. Put stick back inside hole. Let glue dry.

Center fabric over the top of the ball and bring the edges down to stick, covering the ball completely.

Tie satin ribbon or yarn in a small bow around fabric and stick as shown in photo. Trim ends of ribbon.

Fold metallic ribbon with ends together. Glue the ends to the back of the lollipop for hanger.

Hang on your Christmas tree! ☆

Patchwork Tablecloth Has Christmas Covered

UNCOVERING a colorful way to dress the dining table for the holidays led crafter Doris Nowell in circles…until she squared up this cloth! It's based on a traditional quilting design called "Trip Around the World", she points out from her Gerrardstown, West Virginia home.

You can follow her plan or devise a color scheme of your own. Even random patches of fabric from your scrap collection will come together prettily for this project.

Materials Needed:
44-inch-wide 100% cotton fabrics—1/4 yard each of white print for center and two green prints for Rounds 1 and 13; 3/8 yard each of two red prints for Rounds 2 and 11 and two white prints for Rounds 3 and 12; 5/8 yard each of two green prints for Rounds 4 and 10 and a red print for Round 5; 3/4 yard each of two white prints for Rounds 6 and 9, a green print for Round 7 and a red print for Round 8; and 5-1/2 yards of coordinating print for backing
Matching all-purpose thread
Rotary cutter and mat (optional)
Quilter's ruler
Quilter's marking pen or pencil
Standard sewing supplies

Finished Size: Tablecloth is 93-1/2 inches long x 60-1/2 inches wide.

Directions:

Pre-wash all fabrics, washing colors separately. If the water from any fabric is discolored, wash again until the rinse water runs clear. Machine-dry and press all fabrics.

CUTTING: Cut fabrics using rotary cutter and quilter's ruler or mark fabrics using ruler and marker of choice and cut with scissors.

Round 1 indicates the first round around the center square, Round 2 is the second round around the center square and so on.

Cut 6-in. squares for all blocks. Cut squares from the same fabrics for each round and label each as follows:

Cut one white square for the center block. Cut four green squares for Round 1. Cut eight red squares for Round 2. Cut 12 white squares for Round 3. Cut 16 green squares for Round 4. Cut 20 red squares for Round 5. Cut 22 white squares for Round 6.

Cut 22 green squares for Round 7. Cut 22 red squares for Round 8. Cut 20 white squares for Round 9. Cut 16 green squares for Round 10. Cut 12 red squares for Round 11. Cut 8 white squares for Round 12. Cut 4 green squares for Round 13.

LAYOUT: Lay out blocks, starting with white center block, as shown in Layout Diagram below. Add each additional round around the center block, making 17 horizontal rows with 11 blocks in each row.

PIECING: Keeping the rest of the layout intact, pick up first horizontal row and stack blocks in planned order.

With right sides together and an accurate 1/4-in. seam, sew first two blocks together. Add third block, checking to make sure that it is sewn in the correct order. Keep adding blocks until the row is complete.

On wrong side of fabric, press seams together in one direction. Return pieced row to planned layout.

Pick up and sew Row 2. Press seams in opposite direction of Row 1. With right sides together, pin Row 2 to bottom edge of Row 1. Sew rows together, carefully matching seams. Press horizontal seams open.

Continuing in this fashion, piece each row and sew it to the bottom edge of the previous row. Press seams in alter-nate directions as instructed before. Press front after adding final row.

ASSEMBLY: Cut the backing fabric in half crosswise, making two 99-in.-long pieces. Pin the pieces with right sides together and edges matching. Sew the pieces together along one long edge with 1/2-in. seam, making a rectangle approximately 89 in. x 99 in. Press the seam open.

Place backing right side up on a flat surface and smooth out wrinkles. Center pieced tablecloth wrong side up on top of backing. Smooth out wrinkles and pin layers together.

Cut along the outside edge of the pieced tablecloth, trimming away the excess backing.

Sew pieced tablecloth to backing with a 1/4-in. seam, leaving an opening for turning. Trim corners diagonally.

Turn right side out through opening. Turn raw edges of opening in and hand-sew opening closed. Press outside seam.

Using thread to match backing fabric, topstitch around tablecloth 1/4 in. from outside edge.

Top your dining table! ☆

LAYOUT DIAGRAM

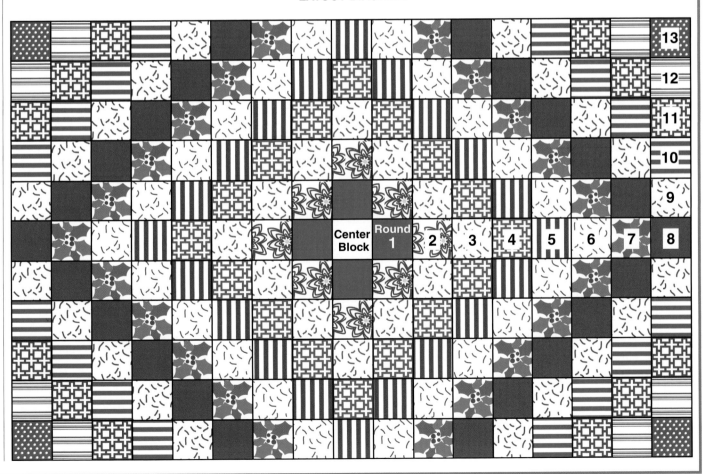

Cardinal Quilt Takes Wing for Christmas

FLOCKS of "oohs" and "aahs" will flutter home when you perch Linda Whitener's pretty cardinal quilt on a wall. Its homespun look is ideal for the holidays…and all winter long.

The bright bird applique is one experienced quilters will find satisfying to make, the Glen Allen, Missouri designer details. "For a bit of extra fun, I used a tree branch from the yard as a hanger," she smiles.

Materials Needed:
Patterns on next page
44-inch-wide 100% cotton fabrics—1/2
yard of muslin for backing; 1/2 yard of white-on-white print for background; 1/4 yard of red narrow-wale corduroy for cardinal; 1/8 yard each of green check for middle border, hanging tabs and holly, dark green print for outer border and holly and dark green solid for inner border; and scraps of brown solid for face, gold solid for beak and brown print for branch
Matching all-purpose thread
1/4 yard of paper-backed fusible web
14-inch x 18-inch piece of lightweight quilt batting
Quilter's marking pen or pencil

Quilter's ruler
Rotary cutter and mat (optional)
Nine red pony beads
Standard sewing supplies
13-inch length of 1/2-inch-diameter tree branch for hanger

Finished Size: Cardinal wall hanging measures about 12 inches wide x 16-1/2 inches high without hanging tabs.

Directions:
Pre-wash fabrics, washing each color separately. If water is discolored, wash again until rinse water runs clear. Dry and press all fabrics.

Do all piecing with accurate 1/4-in. seams and right sides of fabrics together unless instructions say otherwise. Press the seams toward the darker fabric when possible.

CUTTING: Accurately cut the fabrics using rotary cutter and quilter's ruler or mark fabrics using ruler and marker of choice and then cut with scissors. Cut all of the strips crosswise from selvage to selvage.

From white-on-white print, cut a 7-1/2-in. x 12-in. piece for background of appliques.

From dark green solid, cut two 1-in. x 12-in. strips and two 1-in. x 8-1/2-in. strips for inner border.

From green check, cut two 2-in. x 13-in. strips and two 2-in. x 11-1/2-in. strips for middle border. Also cut two 1-1/4-in. x 4-in. pieces for hanging tabs.

From dark green print, cut two 1-in. x 16-in. strips and two 1-in. x 12-1/2-in. strips for outer border.

PIECING: Sew a 1-in. x 12-in. dark green solid border to matching sides of white-on-white background fabric. Then add matching borders to top and bottom edges.

Sew a 2-in. x 13-in. green check border to matching sides. Then add matching borders to top and bottom edges.

Sew a 1-in. x 16-in. green print border to matching sides. Then add matching borders to top and bottom edges.

For hanging tabs, fold each 1-in. x 4-in. green check strip in half lengthwise with right sides together. Stitch long edge with a 1/4-in. seam. Turn each right side out through one open end. Center seams and press each.

Fold each strip in half crosswise with seam inside and raw edges matching. Pin the hanging tabs to the right side of the pieced top with raw edges matching and outside edges of tabs 2 in. from

the side edges of pieced top.

APPLIQUE: Trace individual pattern pieces onto paper side of fusible web as directed on patterns, leaving 1 in. between shapes. Cut shapes apart.

Fuse shapes onto fabrics as directed on patterns, following manufacturer's directions. Cut out the shapes on the traced lines.

Remove paper backing from shapes. Fuse cardinal to white-on-white background fabric as shown in photo. Then add face, beak and branch.

Fuse holly to background fabric as shown in photo, being sure to extend the tip of three of the checked holly leaves onto the inner border.

Shapes will be stitched onto background fabric later.

ASSEMBLY: Place batting on a flat surface and smooth out wrinkles. Center backing right side up on top of batting. Center pieced wall hanging wrong side up on top. Hanging tabs will be sandwiched in between with folds of tabs facing the center. Pin layers together.

Sew around pieced wall hanging 1/4 in. from outside edge of pieced top, leaving an opening for turning along one edge. Trim batting and backing as needed. Clip corners diagonally.

Turn right side out through opening so the batting is sandwiched between the pieced top and the backing. Turn raw edges of opening in and hand-sew opening closed.

QUILTING: With green thread in the needle and off-white thread in the bobbin, stitch around the inner border, stitching 1/8 in. from seam of background and inner border.

Then stitch around middle border, stitching 1/8 in. from seam of inner border and middle border, extending stitching to outer border to form a square in each corner as shown in photo. In same way, stitch around outer border.

APPLIQUE: Do all appliqueing with a medium satin stitch and matching thread as follows: Applique over the inside design lines of the cardinal and then around the outside edges of the cardinal.

Applique around face and then around beak. Stitch eye with gold thread where shown on pattern. Applique around branch and then around each holly leaf, stitching background leaves first. Pull all thread ends to wrong side and secure.

FINISHING: Hand-sew three pony beads to each group of holly where shown in photo.

Insert branch through tabs and hang your Christmas quilt! ☆

CARDINAL WALL HANGING PATTERNS

FACE
Trace 1—paper-backed fusible web
Cut 1—fused brown solid

BEAK
Trace 1—paper-backed fusible web
Cut 1—gold solid

Grain

CARDINAL
Trace 1—paper-backed fusible web
Cut 1—fused red corduroy

BRANCH
Trace 1—paper-backed fusible web
Cut 1—fused brown print

HOLLY
Trace 8—paper-backed fusible web
Cut 4 each—fused green print and fused green check

APPLIQUE KEY
—— Cutting/stitching line
— Inside design line
- - - Under-lap

Note: Patterns are given in reverse so they will face the correct direction after being fused to the back of fabrics.

Fir Holders Glow with Noel Light

PLANT these beaming balsam candle holders among your Christmas trimmings—and they'll surely spark a crop of compliments throughout the season!

Crafter Lana Condon made them for her Jupiter, Florida home, using wooden heart shapes she had on hand. "When I turned the hearts upside down, I immediately envisioned evergreens," she smiles. "They took me just a few hours to finish."

Materials Needed (for both):
Purchased wooden cutouts—two 1/8-inch-thick x 3/4-inch-high hearts, two 1/8-inch-thick x 1-3/4-inch-high hearts, two 1/8-inch-thick x 2-1/2-inch-high hearts, two 1/8-inch-thick x 3-3/4-inch-high hearts, two 1/2-inch-thick x 3-1/2-inch-high hearts and two 3/8-inch-thick x 1-inch stars
Two 1-3/4-inch-high wooden flowerpots
Two brass candle inserts to fit openings of flowerpots
Sandpaper and tack cloth
Paper plate or palette
Acrylic craft paints—brown, gold, green and white
1-inch foam brush
Small piece of household sponge
White (tacky) glue
Two taper candles

Finished Size: Each candle holder without candles is 3-3/4 inches across x 6-1/2 inches high.

Directions:
Sand all wood pieces smooth. Wipe each with tack cloth.

Place small amounts of paints as needed onto paper plate or palette. Paint pieces as instructed below. Add additional coats of paint as needed for complete coverage, allowing drying time between each coat.

Paint 3/4-in.-high hearts brown, stars and 1/2-in.-thick hearts gold and remaining hearts green. Paint flowerpots white. Let dry.

Dip sponge into white and dab paint onto edges of hearts and onto stars as shown in photo. Add a bit of gold to top edge of flowerpots in same way. Let dry.

Glue a flowerpot to center of each gold heart. Let dry.

Referring to photo for placement, glue brown hearts to large green hearts with rounded tops of hearts even.

Glue medium green hearts to same side of large green hearts, placing rounded portion of medium heart over point of large heart. Then glue small green hearts to same side of medium green hearts in the same way. Let dry.

Glue a star to point of each small heart. Glue assembled trees centered to

rounded portion of each gold heart, with bottom of each tree flush with edge of each heart as shown. Let dry.

Glue candle inserts into opening of each flowerpot. Let dry. Place a candle in each holder. ☆

Youngsters Will Cozy Up Quick To This Cute Frosty Fellow!

CHILDREN of all ages just melt when they see this chilly charmer! The soft squeezeable snowman is a perfect fit for small arms.

Amy Albert Bloom of Shillington, Pennsylvania shares the easy instructions for making her cheery stuffed toy. She used fuzzy flannel to construct him, but notes almost any soft material you have on hand will work just fine.

Materials Needed:
Patterns on next page
Tracing paper and pencil
1/2 yard of white flannel
White all-purpose thread

Polyester stuffing
Scraps of black and pink felt
Black 3-ply yarn
Embroidery needle
2-1/2-inch x 20-inch piece of plaid flannel or wool for scarf
Pinking shears (optional)
White (tacky) glue
Standard sewing supplies

Finished Size: Snowman is about 9-1/2 inches tall x 10-1/2 inches across.

Directions:
Trace pattern at right onto tracing paper as directed on pattern.

Fold flannel doubled with right sides

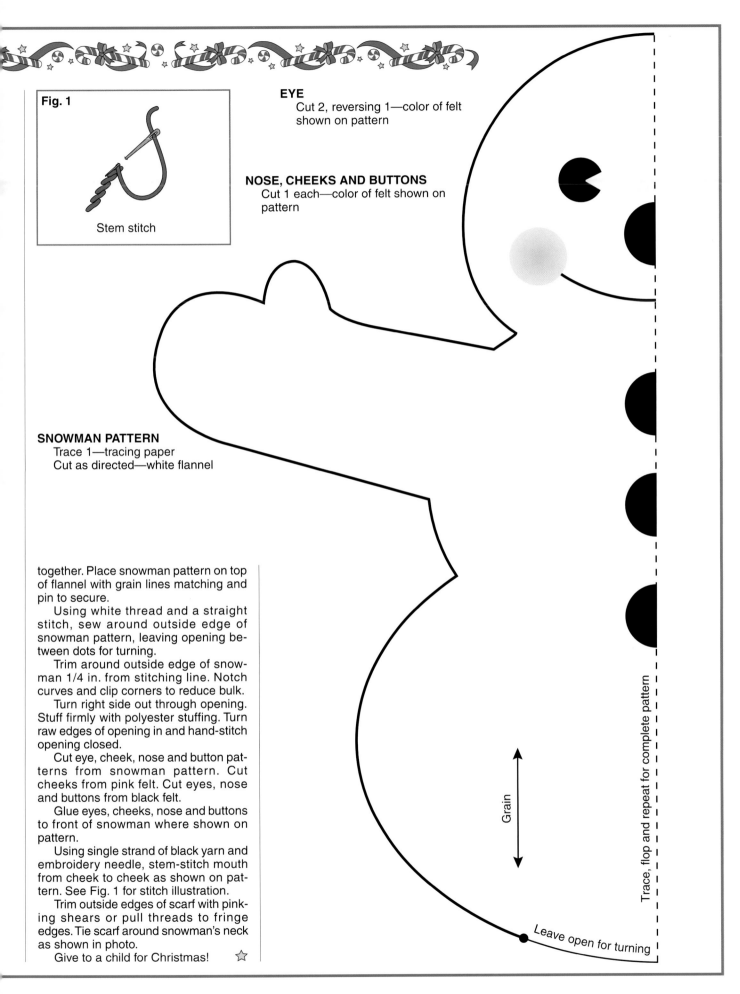

Fig. 1

Stem stitch

EYE
Cut 2, reversing 1—color of felt shown on pattern

NOSE, CHEEKS AND BUTTONS
Cut 1 each—color of felt shown on pattern

SNOWMAN PATTERN
Trace 1—tracing paper
Cut as directed—white flannel

Grain

Trace, flop and repeat for complete pattern

Leave open for turning

together. Place snowman pattern on top of flannel with grain lines matching and pin to secure.

Using white thread and a straight stitch, sew around outside edge of snowman pattern, leaving opening between dots for turning.

Trim around outside edge of snowman 1/4 in. from stitching line. Notch curves and clip corners to reduce bulk.

Turn right side out through opening. Stuff firmly with polyester stuffing. Turn raw edges of opening in and hand-stitch opening closed.

Cut eye, cheek, nose and button patterns from snowman pattern. Cut cheeks from pink felt. Cut eyes, nose and buttons from black felt.

Glue eyes, cheeks, nose and buttons to front of snowman where shown on pattern.

Using single strand of black yarn and embroidery needle, stem-stitch mouth from cheek to cheek as shown on pattern. See Fig. 1 for stitch illustration.

Trim outside edges of scarf with pinking shears or pull threads to fringe edges. Tie scarf around snowman's neck as shown in photo.

Give to a child for Christmas! ☆

Nice-and-Spicy Twosome's Cut Out for Christmas Decorating!

This engaging couple from Bette Veinot of Bridgewater, Nova Scotia will double your fun—whether they garnish the Christmas tree or perk up a shelf.

Bette used wood to "cook up" her crafty gingerbread couple. "These last longer than the traditional baked treats," she offers. "But they're just as sweet!"

Materials Needed (for both):

Patterns on this page
Tracing paper and pencil
3-1/2-inch x 8-inch piece of 3/8-inch-thick pine
Scroll or band saw
Drill with 3/32-inch bit
Sandpaper and tack cloth
Light brown wood stain and soft cloth
Paper plate or palette
Paper towels
Acrylic craft paints—black, red and white
Paintbrushes—small round and liner
Toothpick
7-inch square of striped Christmas fabric
Seam sealant
Five gold seed beads for buttons (optional)
25 inches of green floral wire
Large paper clip
Wire cutters
1-1/2-inch-long miniature wooden rolling pin
4 inches of natural raffia
All-purpose thread to match fabric and raffia
Hand-sewing needle
White (tacky) glue
Scissors

Finished Size: Each ornament is about 3 inches wide x 4 inches tall.

Directions:

Trace patterns onto tracing paper and cut out each.

Trace outline of vest pattern for gingerbread boy once onto wrong side of striped Christmas fabric with a stripe centered down the center front of the vest. Cut out.

From remaining fabric, cut the following pieces, making sure stripes on each run lengthwise: One 3-1/2-in.-wide x 1-1/2-in.-long piece for skirt and two 1/4-in.-wide x 3-1/2-in.-long strips for straps of skirt. Also cut two 1/2-in.-wide x 7-in.-long strips for bows.

Apply seam sealant to edges of all fabric pieces. Let dry.

Trace outline of gingerbread pattern twice onto pine with grainlines matching.

Cut out two gingerbread shapes with scroll or band saw. Drill holes in hands at each "X" on pattern. Sand shapes lightly and wipe with tack cloth to remove sanding dust.

Apply stain with soft cloth. Let dry.

Turn gingerbread pattern over and rub side of pencil lead over inside lines of pattern to darken. Place pattern onto the wood cutout and trace over lines to transfer pattern onto wood. Repeat on other gingerbread shape.

PAINTING: Place small amounts of paint onto paper plate or palette as needed. Paint as directed below.

Dip handle of paintbrush into black and dab eyes on each shape. Let dry.

Mix equal amounts of red paint and water. Dip round brush into mixture and blot excess on paper towel until nearly dry. Then paint cheeks on each ornament. Let dry.

Mix equal amounts of water and black together and use liner to paint eyebrows, eyelashes, nose and mouth on each. Let dry.

Using liner, paint white design lines on each shape, extending lines onto side edges of cutouts. Let dry.

Use toothpick and white paint to dab a tiny dot onto each eye. Let dry.

Referring to pattern for placement, paint a small red heart on top of head and on right leg of each gingerbread

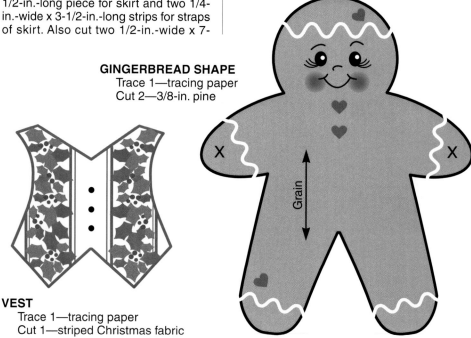

GINGERBREAD SHAPE
Trace 1—tracing paper
Cut 2—3/8-in. pine

VEST
Trace 1—tracing paper
Cut 1—striped Christmas fabric

Grain

X   X

shape. Add two small red hearts under chin for gingerbread girl only. To make hearts, use toothpick to dab on two small red dots of paint as shown in Fig. 1. Then pull down paint from each dot to form point of heart. Let dry.

FINISHING: Glue straps right side up to front of gingerbread girl as shown in photo. Cross straps in back and trim excess. Let dry.

Hand-stitch 1/4 in. from one long edge of skirt to gather edge to fit across front only of gingerbread girl. Fasten off thread. Glue stitched edge of skirt to front of gingerbread girl, covering ends of straps.

Glue the vest right side up to front of gingerbread boy. Let dry.

Cut a 12-1/2-in. piece of floral wire. Open paper clip and straighten wire. Wrap floral wire loosely around wire of paper clip to coil, leaving about 2 in. of floral wire at each end straight. Slide coiled floral wire off paper clip.

Insert straight ends of floral wire from back to front through holes in hands, leaving a hanging loop of coiled wire in back. Then coil floral wire at front of hands as before. Use wire cutter to trim excess. Repeat with remaining floral wire to make hanging loop for other gingerbread trim.

Glue rolling pin to one hand of gingerbread girl. Wrap a bit of coiled wire from hand around handle of rolling pin.

If desired, glue three seed beads down center front of vest and a seed bead to skirt at end of each strap.

Tear raffia lengthwise into six narrow strips. Working with three strips as one, form raffia into a small bow. See Fig. 2. Wrap center of bow with thread. Glue to hold.

Glue the raffia bow to top of skirt as shown in photo. Make another bow as before and glue bow to top of vest.

Tie each 1/2-in.-wide x 7-in.-long fabric strip into a small bow around the hanging loop of each ornament as shown in the photo.

Have fun trimming your tree! ☆

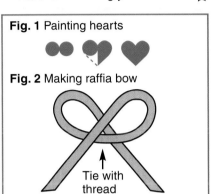

Fig. 1 Painting hearts

Fig. 2 Making raffia bow

Tie with thread

Fancy Fabric Marker Helps Put Words in Place

HERE'S a novel idea for the avid reader on your Christmas list. This festive bookmark will surely rank as a best-seller for both of you.

Not only is it practical, Kentuckian Helen Rafson notes that the colorful page marker is quick to complete, too. "I snipped strips of print fabrics and stitched them together," she details from Louisville. "I was done in no time!"

Materials Needed:
Ten 1-1/4-inch-wide x 8-inch-long strips of fabric in several different red and green Christmas prints
2-3/4-inch x 7-1/2-inch piece of coordinating fabric for backing
Matching all-purpose thread
8-inch square of heavy interfacing
8 inches of 1/4-inch-wide gold metallic ribbon
Standard sewing supplies

Finished Size: Bookmark is about 2-1/4 inches wide x 7 inches long.

Directions:
Place one fabric strip right side up on interfacing with long edges matching.

Place second fabric strip on top of first strip with right sides together and long edges and ends matching. Sew strips together along long inside edge with a 1/4-in. seam. Open and press strip toward interfacing.

Continue to add remaining strips in same way, pressing strips open after each addition.

Fold one short edge of backing diagonally so raw edge matches raw edge of long side. Press lightly to crease fold. Then unfold.

Pin the backing to the pieced strips with right sides together and pressed crease parallel to a seam line of pieced strips. See Fig. 1.

Stitch around the backing 1/4 in. from outside edges, leaving an opening along one long edge for turning. Trim through

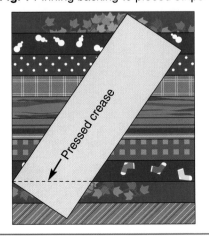

Fig. 1 Pinning backing to pieced strips

Pressed crease

all layers 1/4 in. outside stitching line. Clip corners diagonally.

Turn bookmark right side out through opening. Press raw edges in. Hand-sew opening closed.

Tie metallic ribbon into a small bow. Hand-sew the bow to the narrow end of the bookmark. Trim ends of the bow at an angle to desired length. Tuck inside a favorite holiday book. ☆

Doily Lends a Lacy Look to Holiday Decor

THIS colorfully crocheted doily is certain to "star" in your Christmas decor!

Once you start on the pattern from Emma Willey of Winston, Oregon, you'll likely find yourself hooked. Don't be surprised if you end up with a sky-high pile to give as gifts!

Materials Needed:
Size 10 crochet cotton—one ball each of green, red and white
Size 5 steel crochet hook or size needed to obtain correct gauge
Tapestry needle
Scissors

Finished Size: Doily measures about 20 inches across.

Gauge: End of Round 3 = 2-1/4 inches across from tip to tip of star.

Special Stitches:
2 DOUBLE CROCHET CLUSTER (2Dc-Cl): * Yo, insert hk in the sp indicated and draw up a lp, yo, draw through two lps on hk, repeat from * one more time, yo, draw through all lps on hk.
3 DOUBLE CROCHET CLUSTER (3Dc-Cl): Work 2Dc-Cl, repeating stitches following * one more time, then draw through all lps on hk.
4 DOUBLE CROCHET CLUSTER

(4Dc-Cl): Work 2Dc-Cl, repeating stitches following * two more times, draw through all lps on hk.
3 TREBLE CROCHET CLUSTER (3Tr-Cl): * Yo twice, insert hk in the sp indicated, draw up a lp, [yo, draw through two lps] twice, repeat from * two more times, yo, draw through all lps on hk.
4 TREBLE CROCHET CLUSTER (4Tr-Cl): * Yo twice, insert hk in the sp indicated, draw up a lp, [yo, draw through two lps] twice, repeat from * three more times, yo, draw through all lps on hk.
SHELL (SH): Work (2 dc, ch 1, 2 dc) in space indicated. Work SH of next round in center ch-1 sp.

Directions:
With red, ch 6; join with sl st in beginning ch to form a ring. Work in rounds without turning.

Round 1: Ch 3 (counts as first dc here and throughout), work 23 dcs in ring; join with sl st in third ch of beginning ch-3: 24 dcs.

Round 2: Ch 3, dc in each of next three dcs, ch 2, * dc in each of next four dcs, ch 2; repeat from * around; join with sl st in third ch of beginning ch-3: 24 dcs.

Round 3: Ch 4 for first tr and complete 4Tr-Cl over next three dcs, ch 10, work [4Tr-Cl over next four dcs, ch 10] around; join with sl st in third ch of beginning ch-4. Fasten off: six pointed star with six ch-10 sps.

Round 4: Join green with sl st in top of any 4Tr-Cl and ch 3 for first dc, dc in same 4Tr-Cl, work [12 dcs in next ch-10 sp, dc in next 4Tr-Cl] twice, work 12 dcs in next ch-10 sp, work 2 dcs in next 4Tr-Cl, work [12 dcs in next ch-10 sp, dc in next 4Tr-Cl] twice, work 12 dcs in next ch-10 sp; join with sl st in third ch of ch-3. Fasten off: 80 dcs.

Round 5: Join white with sl st in any dc, ch 4 for first tr and complete 3Tr-Cl over next two dcs, ch 6, sk 1 dc; * work 3Tr-Cl over next 3 dcs, ch 6, sk 1 dc; repeat from * around; join with sl st in top of first cl: 20 3Tr-Cls.

Round 6: Ch 5, dc in next ch-6 sp, ch 2, dc in same sp, ch 2, dc in next 3Tr-Cl; * [ch 2, dc in next ch-6 sp] twice, ch 2, dc in next 3Tr-Cl; repeat from *

around, ending with [ch 2, dc in next ch-6 sp] twice, ch 2; join with sl st in third ch of beginning ch-5.

Round 7: Ch 3 for first dc, [work 2 dcs in next ch-2 sp, dc in next dc] three times, ch 3, sk next ch-2 sp, sc in next ch-2 sp, ch 3, sk next ch-2 sp; * dc in next dc, [work 2 dcs in next ch-2 sp, dc in next dc] three times, ch 3, sk next ch-2 sp, sc in next ch-2 sp, ch 3, sk next ch-2 sp; repeat from * around; join with sl st in third ch of beginning ch-3.

Round 8: Ch 5, * sk 2 dcs, dc in each of next 4 dcs, ch 2, sk 2 dcs, dc in next dc, [ch 3, sc in next ch-3 sp] twice, ch 3, dc in first dc of next group, ch 2; repeat from * around, ending last repeat with ch 3; join with sl st in third ch of beginning ch-5.

Round 9: Ch 5, * work 4Dc-Cl over next 4 dcs, ch 5, sc in next dc, ch 5, sk next ch-sp, work 4Dc-Cl in next ch-sp, ch 5, sk next ch-sp, sc in next dc, ch 5; repeat from * around, ending with sl st in first ch of beginning ch-5.

Rounds 10-12: Sl st to center of first ch-5 sp; * ch 5, sc in next ch-sp; repeat from * around; ch 5; join with sl st in first ch of beginning ch-5.

Round 13: Ch 3 for first dc of SH and complete SH in first ch-sp, ch 4, sc in next ch-sp, ch 4; * work SH in next ch-sp, ch 4, sc in next ch-sp, ch 4; repeat from * around; join with sl st in third ch of beginning ch-3.

Round 14: Sl st to center of next SH, ch 3 for first dc of SH and complete * SH in SH, ch 9, dc in next SH, ch 9; repeat from * around; join with sl st in third ch of beginning ch-3.

Round 15: Sl st to center of next SH, ch 3 for first dc of SH and complete * SH in SH, ch 9, work 3 dcs in next dc, ch 9; repeat from * around; join with sl st in third ch of beginning ch-3.

Round 16: Sl st to center of next SH, ch 3 for first dc of SH and complete * SH in SH, ch 5, sc over next sp catching ch-sp of two previous rounds, ch 5; work 3Dc-Cl over next 3 dcs, ch 5, sc over next sp catching ch-sp of two previous rounds, ch 5; repeat from * around; join with sl st in third ch of beginning ch-3.

Round 17: Sl st to center of next SH, ch 3 for first dc of SH and complete * SH in SH, [ch 5, work 1 sc in next sp] four times, ch 5; repeat from * around; join with sl st in third ch of beginning ch-3.

Round 18: Sl st to center of next SH, ch 3 for first dc and complete * SH in SH, [ch 5, sc in next sp] five times, ch 5; repeat from * around; join with sl st in

third ch of beginning ch-3. Fasten off.

Round 19 (stars): With red, ch 6; join with sl st in beginning ch to form a ring. Work Rounds 1-3, fastening star to outside edge of doily in Round 3 as follows: Ch 4 for first tr and complete 4Tr-Cl over next three dcs, ch 10; work 4Tr-Cl over next four dcs, ch 5 and with wrong sides together, sc in third sp to left of any SH, ch 5, work 4Tr-Cl over next 4 dcs of star, ch 5, sc in third sp to the right of next shell, ch 5; * work 4Tr-Cl over next 4 dcs of star, ch 10; repeat from * two more times; join with sl st in top of first cl; fasten off. Repeat Round 19 nine more times, adding a total of 10 stars to doily.

Round 20: Join white with sl st in center ch-sp of any SH, * ch 7, sc in first open ch-10 sp of next star, ch 7, sc in same ch-sp, [ch 7, sc in next ch-sp, ch 7, sc in same ch-sp] three times, ch 7, sc in center ch-sp of next SH; repeat from * around, replacing final ch-7 with ch 3, tr in beginning st.

Round 21: * Ch 7, sc in next ch-sp; repeat from * around, replacing final ch-7 with ch 3, tr in top of previous tr.

Round 22: Repeat Round 21.

Round 23: * Ch 3, work 2Dc-Cl over next 2 sps, ch 3, sc in next sp [ch 9, sc in next sp] six times; repeat from * around; join with sl st in top of previous tr. Fasten off.

Round 24: Join green with sl st in first ch-9 sp of any scallop, ch 3 for first dc, work (5 dc, ch 3, sl st in first ch, 6 dc) in same ch-sp, sc in next sc, work * [(6 dc, ch 3, sl st in first ch, 6 dc) in next ch-sp, sc in next sc] five times, work [4 dc in next ch-3 sp] twice, sc in next sc; repeat from * around; join with sl st in first ch of beginning ch-3. Fasten off. Weave in loose ends. ☆

ABBREVIATIONS

ch(s)	chain(s)
cl(s)	cluster(s)
dc(s)	double crochet(s)
hk	hook
lp(s)	loop(s)
sc(s)	single crochet(s)
sk	skip or skipped
sl st	slip stitch
sp(s)	space(s)
st(s)	stitch(es)
tr	treble crochet
yo	yarn over
* or [ ]	Instructions following asterisk or within brackets are repeated as directed.
( )	Instructions in parentheses are all worked in one stitch or space as indicated.

Kids Get a Kick Out of St. Nick!

THIS jolly fellow hauls in big grins when youngsters set out to make him. The project requires simple supplies, like the lid from a frozen juice can to form his face and yarn for his hair, confirms Kaci Ogg of Omaha, Nebraska.

"It's a nice craft to share with a Girl Scout troop or 4-H group," she smiles. "He makes a fine fridgie or pin as well as a tree trim."

Materials Needed:

Pattern on this page
Tracing paper and pencil
5-inch x 7-inch piece of red felt
2-5/8-inch-diameter metal lid from frozen juice can
Acrylic craft paints—black, flesh and white
Small flat paintbrush
Toothpick
Small amount of polyester stuffing or cotton ball
1/2-inch jingle bell
6mm red faceted bead or pom-pom
5-inch square of heavy cardboard
5 yards of worsted-weight white yarn
Gold metallic thread for hanger
Hand-sewing needle
White (tacky) glue
Scissors

Finished Size: Santa trim measures about 4 inches across x 5 inches high.

Directions:

Wash and dry lid. Paint top of lid flesh. Let dry.

Trace hat pattern onto tracing paper. Cut hat from piece of red felt as directed on pattern.

Place opened hat piece on a flat surface with wrong side up. Glue lid, painted side up, onto hat where shown on pattern. Fold and glue right edge of hat over top of lid with edges matching. Glue raw edges together.

Paint black eyes onto lid below hat as shown in photo. When dry, dip toothpick into white and dab a small dot onto each eye.

Glue polyester stuffing or stretched-out cotton ball along bottom edge of hat for fur trim.

Cut a 10-in. piece of yarn and set it aside. Wrap remaining yarn around cardboard. Slide yarn off cardboard. Tie looped yarn in center with 10-in. piece of yarn to secure. Trim ends as needed.

Glue yarn to lid below eyes for beard as shown in photo. Glue red bead or pom-pom to lid above the beard.

Fold tip of hat down using fold line as a guide and glue tip to yarn beard on the right side of the beard. Glue bell to tip of hat.

Hand-sew a loop of gold metallic thread centered to top of hat for hanger. ☆

Place on fold of felt

Fold

HAT PATTERN
Trace 1—tracing paper
Cut 1—folded red felt

Glue lid here

Merry Sweatshirt Sports Christmas Character

BEARING the convincing message to "Always Believe!", this Santa-enhanced sweatshirt packs plenty of fun for a young one at Christmas.

"The design is a nice one to paint, particularly for more experienced crafters," confides designer Annie Lang of Grand Blanc, Michigan. "You can also brush this cheery motif onto a canvas tote bag if you like."

Materials Needed:
Pattern on next page
Tracing paper and pencil
Fabric transfer pen or pencil
White cotton/polyester-blend
  sweatshirt
Paper plate or palette
Paper towels
Container of water
Acrylic fabric paints (or acrylic craft
  paints and textile medium)—antique
  gold, black, bright green, Christmas
  green, Christmas red, flesh, light
  blue, white and yellow

Paintbrushes—Nos. 2
  and 4 flat, Nos. 2 and 4
  round and 5/0 liner
T-shirt board or heavy
  cardboard to fit inside
  sweatshirt
Waxed paper
Straight pins
Iron and ironing surface

Finished Size: Design is about 5-3/4 inches wide x 8-3/4 inches high and is shown painted on a Child size Small sweatshirt.

Directions:
Pre-wash and dry sweatshirt, following manufacturer's instructions. Do not use detergents with built-in stain resistors or fabric softeners. Press if needed.

Trace pattern onto tracing paper. Turn pattern over and retrace over pattern using transfer pen or pencil. Do not retrace lettering with transfer pen or pencil at this time.

Place pattern right side up centered on right side of sweatshirt front. Top point of star should be about 1/2 in. below band at neck of sweatshirt.

Pin pattern in place. Transfer pattern to front of sweatshirt, following transfer pen or pencil instructions.

Place a piece of waxed paper over T-shirt board or cardboard to protect surface. With right side out, slip sweatshirt over T-shirt board or cardboard. Smooth sweatshirt and pin sleeves out of the way. Place sweatshirt on a flat surface.

PAINTING: Place small amounts of each paint on paper plate or palette as needed. If necessary, mix paints with textile medium prior to use.

Paint all areas with full-strength paint unless directed otherwise. Use appropriate size brush for each area to be painted.

Star: Use flat brush to basecoat star with yellow. While paint is still wet, apply a bit of antique gold with flat brush to the outside edges and the "fold" lines to shade. Let dry.

Use round brush to paint tongue and nose Christmas red. Thin a bit of Christmas red with a tiny amount of water. Apply thinned color to each cheek area

with round brush and a circular motion. Let dry.

Use flat brush to fill in mouth with black. Let dry.

Use liner and black to add each eye, outline nose and add details to mouth. Let dry.

Santa: Use flat brush and flesh to paint Santa's face. Let dry.

Use round brush to paint nose and tongue Christmas red. Thin a bit of Christmas red with a tiny amount of water. Apply thinned color to each cheek area with round brush and a circular motion. Let dry.

Use flat brush to paint the inside of mouth black. Let dry.

Use liner and black to add each eye and to outline nose.

Use flat brush and red to paint hat, coat, three stripes on shirt and two stripes on each leg.

Mix a bit of black with Christmas red to make a dark red for shading. Apply the dark red near the beard and fur of coat and to hat and sleeves to shade where shown on pattern. Also add dark red shading to "fold" lines of coat.

Use flat brush and black to paint Santa's mittens.

Use round brush and light blue to paint edges of beard and all fur trim with a circular motion. While paint is still wet, paint over areas with white.

Use flat brush and light blue to paint side edges of unpainted stripes on shirt and left edges of legs to shade. While paint is still wet, apply white over stripes. Let dry.

Use flat brush and bright green to paint shoes and banners. While paint is still wet, apply Christmas green to edges to shade.

FINISHING: Use flat brush and white to highlight right side of shirt, mittens, shoes and cuffs where shown on the pattern.

Use liner and white to add tiny highlights to each nose, cheek and down center of each leg. Let dry.

Use transfer pen or pencil to retrace lettering onto the back of the pattern. Transfer the lettering onto the banners as directed before.

Use round brush to paint lettering black.

Use liner and black to outline and add all details as shown on pattern. Thin black paint with a bit of water as needed to keep paint flowing smoothly.

Present to a favorite youngster for Christmas! ☆

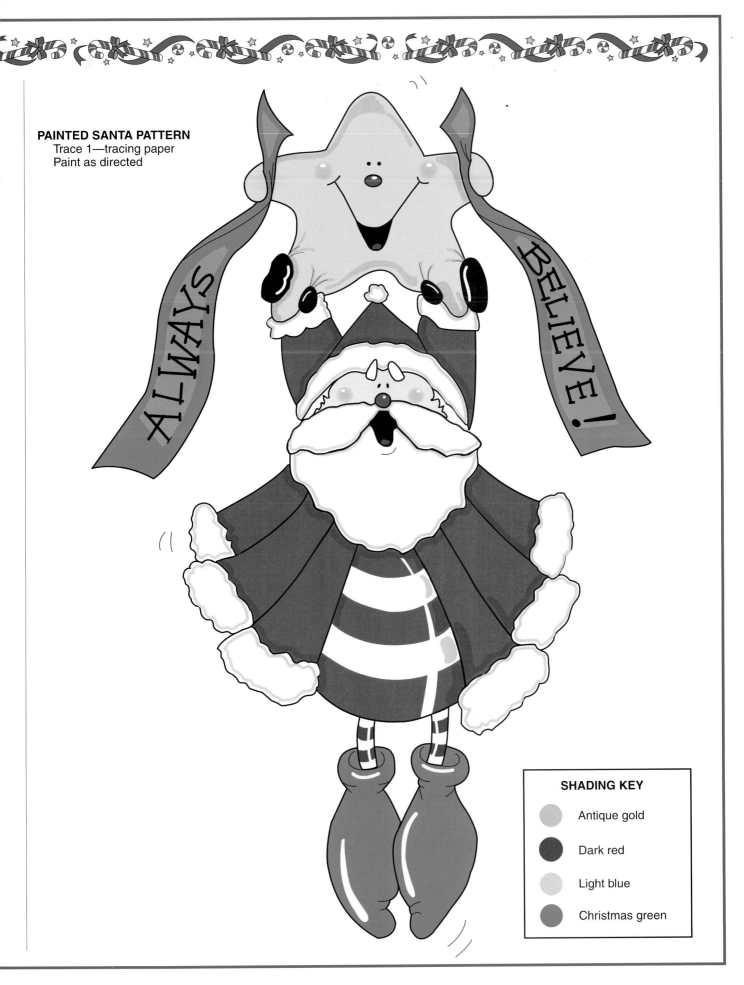

PAINTED SANTA PATTERN
Trace 1—tracing paper
Paint as directed

ALWAYS

BELIEVE!

SHADING KEY

Antique gold

Dark red

Light blue

Christmas green

Stitched Set Will Keep Baby Snug as a Bug

WHEN you bundle up an infant for the elements in this hat and mitten set, Old Man Winter doesn't stand a chance!

The cozy combination from Beverly Blankenbaker of Harvard, Illinois chases chills with flair, thanks to the afghan knit stitch she chose to crochet it. "The stitch is pretty, cuddly and easy to do," notes Beverly.

Materials Needed (for both):
One 3-1/2 ounce skein of off-white worsted-weight 4-ply yarn
Size G/6 (4.5mm) crochet hook
Size H/8 (5mm) afghan hook (a long crochet hook)
3-inch square of cardboard
Tapestry or yarn needle
Scissors

Gauge: Working in afghan knit stitch, 4 sts and 4 rows = 1 inch.

Finished Size: Directions for hat and mittens are for Infant size 6-12 months. Changes for size 18 months are in parentheses. Hat measures about 18 inches around and is about 6-1/2 inches high without tassel. Mittens are about 6 inches around the palm and are about 4 inches long.

Special Stitches:
Afghan crochet is worked using an afghan hook.

Each row is worked in two parts. First the loops are drawn onto the hook and then they are worked off the hook.

AFGHAN FOUNDATION STITCH:
First half: Using afghan hk, pick up the number of sts required. Insert the hk into first st from front to back, yo and draw up a lp. Keeping all lps on hk, draw up a lp in each specified st across. Do not turn work.

Second half: To work lps off, yo and draw through 1 lp, * yo and draw through 2 lps; repeat from * across until only 1 lp remains on the hk. The last lp on the hk is the first lp of the next row. Do not turn work.

This row forms the foundation of the afghan stitch.

AFGHAN KNIT STITCH:
Work first and second half of afghan foundation stitch and then work first and second half of afghan knit stitch as follows to complete one row of afghan knit stitch:

First half: Holding yarn to back of work skip first vertical bar; *insert hk between next set of vertical bars and under ch to back of work, draw up a lp to front of work; keeping all lps on hk, repeat from * across.

Second half: Yo and draw through 1 lp, * yo and draw through 2 lps; repeat from * across until only 1 lp remains on the hk. Retain lp for start of next row.

After a few rows, your work will have the appearance of stockinette knitting.

Directions:
HATBAND: Row 1: With crochet hk, ch 5, work 1 sc in second ch from hk and in each ch across, ch 1, turn: 4 scs.

Rows 2-62 (2-66): Working in back lps only, sc in each sc across, ch 1, turn. At end of Row 62 (66) retain lp of last sc. Do not turn.

HAT: Row 1: With afghan hk, work afghan foundation stitch, working in end of each sc row of hatband: 63 (67) sts.

Rows 2-21 (2-26): Work afghan knit stitch.

Row 22 (27): Work first half of afghan knit stitch row. For second half, yo and draw through 2 lps, * yo and draw through 3 lps; repeat from * across, leaving 1 lp on hk.

Rows 23-24 (28-29): Repeat Row 22 (27), working grouped sts from Row 22 (27) as one st and leaving 1 lp on hk.

Cut yarn, leaving a 30-in.-long tail of yarn. Yo and pull yarn through last lp. Using tapestry or yarn needle, weave yarn through last row made. Draw up yarn tightly to gather top of hat.

Fold hat with right sides together and stitch seam with tapestry needle and tail of yarn, matching ends of rows. Fasten off and weave in loose ends. Turn hat right side out.

POM-POM: Wrap yarn around 3-in. square of cardboard about 75 times. Carefully remove yarn from cardboard. Tie loops of yarn together tightly in middle with a scrap of yarn, leaving a tail of yarn. Cut through loops at both ends. Fluff pom-pom and trim yarn as needed. Sew pom-pom to center top of hat.

MITTENS (make two): BAND: Row 1: With crochet hk, ch 5, work 1 sc in second ch from hk and in each ch across, ch 1, turn: 4 scs.

Rows 2-20 (2-24): Working in back lps only, sc in each sc across, ch 1, turn. At end of Row 20 (24) retain lp of last sc. Do not turn.

HAND: Row 1: With afghan hk, work afghan foundation stitch, working in ends of sc rows of band: 21 (25) sts.

Rows 2-12 (2-16): Work afghan knit stitch.

Row 13 (17): Work first half of afghan knit stitch row. For second half, yo and draw through 2 lps; * yo and draw through 3 lps; repeat from * across, leaving 1 lp on hk.

Row 14 (18): Repeat Row 13 (17), working grouped sts from Row 13 (17)

ABBREVIATIONS	
ch(s)	chain(s)
hk	hook
lp(s)	loop(s)
sc(s)	single crochet(s)
sl st	slip stitch
st(s)	stitch(es)
yo	yarn over

as one st and leaving 1 lp on hk.

Cut yarn, leaving a 24-in.-long tail of yarn. Yo and pull yarn through last lp. Using tapestry or yarn needle, weave yarn through last row made. Draw up yarn tightly to gather tip of mitten.

Fold mitten with right sides together and stitch seam, using tapestry needle and tail of yarn. Fasten off and weave in loose ends. Turn mitten right side out.

MITTEN CORD: Using crochet hk, attach yarn in seam of first mitten with a sc; ch to make a 30-in.-long cord. Attach cord to seam of second mitten with 2 scs, turn, sl st in each ch across to first mitten; work 1 sc in seam of first mitten, sl st in first sc. Fasten off.

Cozy up baby with your handiwork!

Candy Figures into Yule Flavor

HOW SWEET! These clever characters will enliven your table and serve as tasty tidbits, too. And most delicious of all, they are super quick and easy to make!

"Just pile up a few foil-wrapped candies, tape them together and add easy embellishments," explains Leslie Hartsock of Bartlesville, Oklahoma. "This is a craft kids really enjoy doing," she adds.

Materials Needed (for all):
Christmas foil-wrapped candies—
 Reese's Miniature Peanut
 Butter Cups, Hershey's Chocolate
 Kisses and Hershey's Rolos
Double-coated tape with permanent
 adhesive on both sides
Scissors

Materials Needed (for each tree):
One gold foil-wrapped Rolo
Two green foil-wrapped peanut
 butter cups
One green foil-wrapped
 chocolate kiss
Treetop trim—1/2-inch star button or 8

inches of 1/8-inch-wide or 1/4-inch-wide satin ribbon

Materials Needed (for each reindeer):
Two gold or red foil-wrapped peanut
 butter cups
One green or brown pipe cleaner
 (chenille stem)
Two 7mm flat-backed wiggle eyes
One 1/8-inch red pom-pom

Materials Needed (for each Santa):
One red foil-wrapped peanut butter cup
Two gold foil-wrapped Rolos
One red foil-wrapped chocolate kiss
Two 7mm flat-backed wiggle eyes
One 1/4-inch red pom-pom
Two cotton balls

Materials Needed (for each elf):
One red or green foil-wrapped
 peanut butter cup
Two gold foil-wrapped Rolos
One red or green foil-wrapped
 chocolate kiss
Two 7mm flat-backed wiggle eyes

One 1/4-inch red pom-pom
3/8-inch-wide x 6-inch-long piece of
 red or green Christmas print fabric

Finished Size: Each candy character is about 3 inches tall x 1-1/2 inches wide.

Directions:
TREE: Using a small piece of double-coated tape, attach the flat end of the chocolate kiss to narrow end of the peanut butter cup.

Add another peanut butter cup with narrow end up to bottom of first peanut butter cup in the same way. Tape second peanut butter cup to narrow end of Rolo to make tree shape.

Tape star button to top of tree. Or tie ribbon into a small bow and tape it to tree as shown in photo.

REINDEER: Tape the wide ends of two peanut butter cups together with the edges matching.

Cut pipe cleaner in half and wrap each piece around a pencil, making a coil about 1-1/2 in. long. Remove pipe cleaner from pencil. Fasten coiled pipe cleaners to top peanut butter cup for antlers as shown in photo.

Use small pieces of tape to adhere wiggle eyes and pom-pom nose to top peanut butter cup.

SANTA: Using small pieces of double-coated tape, adhere the wide ends of two Rolos together with edges matching. Center and tape the narrow end of a peanut butter cup to narrow end of one Rolo for bottom of Santa. Tape a chocolate kiss to the top Rolo for Santa's hat.

Use small pieces of tape to attach wiggle eyes and pom-pom nose to top Rolo as shown in photo.

Shape cotton ball into a beard and mustache as shown in photo. Use small pieces of tape to attach to head.

ELF: Assemble candies as instructed for Santa.

Add wiggle eyes and pom-pom nose.

Wrap fabric strip around candies as shown in photo. Make 1/2-in.-long cuts 1/8 in. apart at each end of fabric strip for fringe. Secure the ends with double-coated tape.

Tuck the festive figures on a table or in a stocking! ☆

This Crafter's Colorful Signs Deliver a Very Merry Message

ALL THE SIGNS point to Christmas in Karen Marti's workshop.

From a Nativity door-topper bearing the message "Peace on Earth" to a rustic Santa wall hanging, cheery country cherubs and more, the space simply brims with good cheer.

"I love to create and paint wooden Christmas trims," Karen beams about the crafty enterprise she operates with husband Mike from their Middleton, Wisconsin home.

The writing's not only on the wall—this imaginative lady's also dreamed up a whole grove of holiday garnishes meant to brighten everything from tabletops to tree limbs.

"I like to create pretty but practical items, such as a cardinal-topped basket that's perfect for holding greeting cards…or country clocks accented with merry scenes of Santa and his sleigh," Karen explains.

"For inspiration, I just look out the window of our walk-in basement studio and enjoy the 2 acres of woods beyond. Antiques often give me ideas, as well."

Once a concept's taken shape in her mind, Mike cuts it out of pine. Then Karen paints the adornments in colorful country hues. "The last step is adding little touches like buttons to brighten a pine tree or fabric scarves and frocks to warm up Christmas snowmen and angels.

"Working together is such fun," Karen shares. "Mike and I've been crafting like this ever since we were first married. Back then, we did it as a way to give meaningful holiday gifts and to brighten our small apartment.

"After a while, friends encouraged us to sell our wood designs at a local craft show…and the response was overwhelming," Karen recalls. "Things just kept growing after that."

Indeed, these days Karen and Mike turn out wooden country trims by the trunkful from their rural abode. Other holidays besides Christmas are represented, too, but Noel notions are always at the top of the list.

"Come spring, we're already buzzing with December projects," notes Karen. "Thankfully, we have a handful of local folks who help us out regularly.

"Even my mom pitches in. Our children, Nathan and Melissa, are both in college so they don't have as much time

SIGNS OF THE TIMES, from wood angels to snowmen, Nativities and wintry villages, all fill Karen Marti's workshop year-round.

to help. But they provide plenty of moral support!

"So do folks when they tell us how they enjoy our designs," Karen smiles. "And that's possibly the best gift of all!"

Editor's Note: *For a color catalog of her woodcrafts, write to Karen at Homestead Creations, 4920 Highwood Cir., Middleton WI 53562. Or call 1-800/362-6035.* ☆

Doll House Sets a Festive Holiday Scene

THERE'S no doubt about it. Betty LaFollette Johnson of Griswold, Iowa loves getting her shop all dolled up for the holidays!

Betty is the owner of the Doll House, a 110-year-old cottage that's home to more than 800 dolls dating from the 1800s to the present. She collects old dolls and repairs those in need of a little tender loving care.

This time of year, the gracious grandmother is busy setting a merry scene—with pretty poinsettias, evergreen swags and festively dressed dolls poised to enjoy seasonal activities.

In the living room, for instance, dolls crowd to listen as another in a rocker reads *The Night Before Christmas*. Nearby, pajama-clad friends arrange garlands on a tree.

Dressed in festive finery, porcelain dolls in a Victorian room hold gaily wrapped presents, trim an ornate tree and enjoy a small tea party.

Visitors who look closely are sure to recognize old favorites, like Nancy Ann Storybook and Chatty Cathy dolls.

"Folks often point out a doll they had, or wished they had, as a child. They bring back such memories," smiles Betty, who's also designed her own line of pioneer dolls to commemorate historic trail rides by early Americans.

Most of the action in the Doll House these days, however, hails from the kitchen, where child-size dolls standing 36 inches high are posed participating in holiday preparations.

In one corner, a doll sews candy cane curtains while another adds gingerbread lights and candy canes to a tree. At the

LITTLE DARLINGS delight young and old at the Doll House shop where owner Betty La-Follette Johnson (above) primps for season.

kitchen table, a blonde with ringlets stirs up a batch of cookies while a curly-headed friend rolls out dough.

Besides Christmas, Betty dresses her dolls for other themes during the year. She also changes displays as dolls are sold. But she has hundreds waiting in the wings to repair before they can be displayed and "adopted".

"I love taking a doll in bad shape and making it beautiful," Betty shares. "People are so happy when I've restored their own or their grandmother's doll. A hug of thanks from them makes my day."

Editor's Note: *The Doll House, 810 Main St., is at the intersection of highways 48 and 92 in Griswold, Iowa. It's open from 10 a.m. to 5 p.m. Wednesday to Saturday from April through December. Admission is free. For more information, write to the Doll House, P.O. Box 656, Griswold IA 51535; 1-712/778-4332.* ☆

There's Room at Her Inn for the Holidays

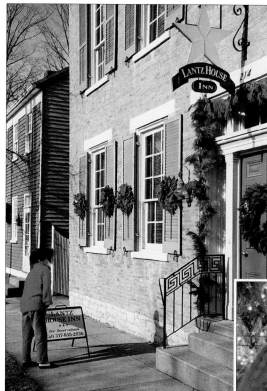

"INN" STEP with the season is nostalgic bed-and-breakfast retreat Marcia Hoyt (in apron above) runs. It's all decked out for the holidays with pine boughs and wreaths draping the entry, antique ornaments trimming the tree and mouth-watering aromas wrapping house in warmth.

HOOSIER HOSPITALITY is perennially present in Centerville, Indiana where Marcia Hoyt's cozy bed-and-breakfast is the "inn" place to be.

"I go all out during the year to make my Lantz House Inn inviting," Marcia confides. "But at Christmastime, I roll out the red carpet…along with poinsettias, festive tablecloths and a 10-foot fir tree by the fireplace.

"Besides accommodating overnight guests, I hostess holiday lunches and dinners for groups," she explains how she caters to all kinds of company in her renovated 1823 Federal-style brick building that's on the National Register of Historic Places.

"Since preparing for these festive occasions is half the fun, my mother, friends and their families come to help me with decorating."

Beginning the day after Thanksgiving, Marcia decks her halls, walls and staircase with greens, pinecones, candles and ribbons. The tree is dressed in antique ornaments from her collection, and doors are spruced up with wreaths.

Tasteful trimming is only part of a full menu of duties Marcia assumes as innkeeper, however. "My meals feature fillets, chicken, homemade bread, gourmet salads and chocolate and white mousse pies," the avid cook lists.

"I've welcomed bridge clubs, sororities, women's groups and family reunions that enjoy getting together in old-fashioned surroundings. Once, the German Heritage Society met here for an array of Bavarian desserts topped off by German Christmas carols.

"After dinner, when we're gathered around the fireplace munching Christmas cookies, I often tell visitors about the history of this building. Its original owner, Daniel Lantz, built prized Conestoga wagons here and outfitted hundreds of pioneers heading west."

Heading to her inn each December has become a holiday tradition for some of her guests, Marcia confirms. "For me, it's like having dear family—scattered across the country—come home for the holidays."

Editor's Note: *If you'd like information or to make reservations, write Marcia at Historic Lantz House Inn, 214 Old National Rd., Centerville IN 47330 or call 1-800/495-2689.* ☆

Old-World Santas Come to Life in Her Crafty Workshop

WE ALL KNOW the real Santa's workshop is located at the North Pole. But another one has been discovered a bit south of there, at East Ootsa in a remote corner of British Columbia.

It's in this secluded spot, 25 miles from the nearest phone and 2-1/2 hours from the closest village, that Gail Begg fashions scraps of wire, wool, fabric and fur into old-world Santas.

"I create them to share all the warm and benevolent feelings that come with Christmas," Gail relates merrily. "I know these fellows are heirlooms that parents and children alike will adore year after year."

Indeed, her Santas have found happy homes all over the world, including the U.S., Finland, Denmark, Germany, Switzerland, Japan and South Africa, Gail confirms.

Much of the appeal of her carefully crafted Kris Kringles lies in their distinctive personalities.

"Each is one-of-a-kind," Gail notes. "The soft sculpture face lends a different expression to every one. Some look stern, some are surprised, some seem lost in thought. It all depends on how I place the eyes, eyebrows and dimples," she explains.

Santas dressed in full-length robes are the simplest to create and take Gail about 6 hours to make. This includes fashioning a head from fiberfilled nylon netting, shaping a body from wire and

wood, sewing clothing and adding Yuletide accessories.

More complicated St. Nicks, like those with clay hands or handmade leather moccasins, can take from 10 to 16 hours to complete. One such series of Santas that appear poised for flight on the back of a swan was inspired by Gail's scenic surroundings.

"That idea came to me one day when I was watching swans and geese fly overhead at Christmastime, hopping from lake to lake," she recalls.

The 85 acres of pristine wilderness surrounding her family's ranch also furnishes many of the accents Gail uses to give her Santas character.

On occasion, daughters Jolene, 19, and Erinn, 15, join her on outings to gather pinecones, willow, moss, lichen, tree mushrooms and more. Husband Marty, who runs a cattle ranch, helps by making wooden stands to mount some of her Santas.

"It's so satisfying to take bits of nature's offerings, a yard of fabric and a strip or two of fur and turn it into something that you know is going to give someone a good feeling every time they look at it," Gail smiles.

Editor's Note: *For a brochure, send $1 to Gail Begg, Artlandish Collectibles, RR2 S14B C5, Burns Lake, BC Canada V0J 1E0. Or contact Gail by phone, 1-250/692-8701, or fax, 1-250/694-3503.* ☆

JOLLY WORKSHOP in East Ootsa, British Columbia is ho-ho-home of crafter Gail Begg (above), where she merrily makes colorful soft-sculpture Kris Kringles with loving care.

I'll Never Forget...

A Special Delivery Helped Keep Christmas in My Heart

By Vicki Henry of Parker, Colorado

THE CHRISTMAS I was 7, my faith in Santa was put to the test. We lived over 300 miles from my grandparents, but Mom insisted that we were driving there for Christmas.

When we'd gone just a few miles from home, I realized that Santa would not know where to deliver my gifts.

"Oh, I'm sure he'll figure it out," my mother assured me.

"But how?" I wailed desperately. "How will he know?"

For the entire trip, I whined and cried. I was miserable and, needless to say, I made sure my parents were miserable, too. After all—it was their fault I would be present-less this Christmas.

Arriving at Granny and Grandpa's, I rushed into the house. There it was—Granny Lehr's aluminum tree with the revolving four-light wheel turning it from red to green to blue to yellow. Not a single gift lay beneath the tree late this Christmas Eve. I was heartbroken.

"Now, don't you worry," Granny soothed as the family filed behind me into the living room.

"Santa doesn't know where you live," I sniffed.

"Why, sure he does! Don't Grandpa and I get Christmas presents every year?" she asked cheerfully.

"You may get something, but he won't know *I'm* here," I insisted.

"You'd better watch your tongue," my stern grandpa warned. "Santa hasn't overlooked a child here in 30 years."

Later that evening as I lay on the floor, chin in my hands, morosely watching the changing colors of the tin tree, Granny shot forward in her rocker. "What's that?" she asked sharply.

I raised up, startled. "What?"

"That noise!" she insisted.

"I heard it, too," Mom confirmed.

They both stood abruptly. "Did you hear bells?" Granny asked my mom, a frown convincing me this was serious.

"Yes. Bells…and yelling."

Granny nodded and pursed her lips. "Santa!" she proclaimed.

My heart raced. The hairs were standing up on my arms. My little brother began to cry.

"Shhhh!" Granny warned. "If it *is* Santa Claus, we can't let him know we're awake!"

Mom and Granny hustled my brother and me into a nearby bedroom. Granny lifted the lace curtain panel from a window and peered out. "I don't see anything," she said.

We all hurried over. I strained to see. Then I heard it. An unmistakable *Thump!* on the roof. The jingling of a harness bell. A deep throaty, "Whoa, there, Dancer! Whoa, boy!"

"It's Santa!" I hissed excitedly at my mother in the dark bedroom.

"I think it is," she whispered back.

More thumps. And jingling. Reindeer were prancing restlessly on the roof. I was so focused on the sounds from above that the creak of Granny's front door opening made me jump.

He was in the house! I could hear boxes sliding…and footsteps right outside my very door! A mere 10 feet separated me from those heavy black boots I heard walking right toward the tree.

Suddenly the noises from the living room ceased. The door hinge squeaked once more, and Santa was back on the roof. Eight reindeer flicked their harness bells one last time as they leaped into the air. The sleigh lightly scraped the shingles and Santa laughed loud and deep, "Merry Christmas!"

Then silence.

We all let out our breath at once. (I'd swear, even today, that Mom and Granny had been holding theirs, too.)

"I think it's safe to go out and look now," Granny nodded.

We quietly ventured out into the living room…and I was awestruck at what I saw—Granny's revolving color wheel cast its light across a pile of brightly wrapped packages.

Grandpa came inside, shaking his head. "I thought I heard somethin', but there wasn't anybody out there," he said.

"You missed them!" I cried.

"Missed them?" he asked.

"Santa and his reindeer! Look!" I showed him proof—packages stacked in a circle beneath the tree.

"How'd I miss that?" he puzzled.

"He was on the roof," I explained. "Didn't you look up?"

Grandpa pushed back the bill of his old Caterpillar cap and rubbed his forehead. "I didn't think of that," he confessed with a twinkle in his eye.

All these years later, I remember that special night—when, thanks to a few loving grown-ups, I kept on believing in the magic of Christmas. ☆

Christmas Parade Lights Up Countryside

By Deborah Quaile of Rockwood, Ontario

WHEN IT COMES to making spirits bright for the holidays, Bev Davis does just that—in a delightful way!

The Ontario farm wife and her husband, Art, spark the season by organizing the area's Parade of Lights, featuring farm equipment floats all decked out in strings of twinkling bulbs, glittering garlands, baubles and bows!

"Along with 10 other families, we dress up about 20 pieces of machinery—from hay wagons, forklifts and balers to cattle trucks and antique tractors," explains the merry matron. "Then we drive through nearby Rockwood as a way to say 'happy holidays' to everyone."

Powered by portable generators strapped onto each piece of equipment, the lights turn everyday implements into glowing sights as they rumble through town after sundown.

Adding a high note, some farmers plug in tape players and broadcast music, while other "elves" hand out candy to the crowd.

Dressed up as Santa and Mrs. Claus, Art and Bev perch on their red Case combine that's been transformed into Santa's sleigh. The couple ties Art's father's horse cutter onto the front of the combine, then daughters Jackie and Debbie help trim the dashing vehicle with hundreds of lights.

"Lastly, we attach spruce roping, wire stars wrapped in lights and big velvet ribbons all around," Bev beams. "Other folks add Christmas trees, wreaths and wooden cutout characters to their farm floats—the sky's the limit!

"It's truly a family affair," Bev informs. "We started the parade back in 1993 to spread Yuletide cheer. Everyone enjoyed it so much, it's become an annual event.

"Last year, some 10,000 people lined the streets to watch us 'parade' by," she chuckles. "Folks come from all over.

"What I find so rewarding is seeing the smiles on youngsters' faces…and knowing that the whole community shares in the spirit of the season."

Editor's Note: *The 8th annual Parade of Lights is tentatively slated to take place December 14, 2000 at 7 p.m. in Rockwood, located on Highway 7. For up-to-date details, contact Deborah Quaile at 1-519/856-2386 or Ian Clark at 1-519/856-2451.* ☆

TAKING A SHINE to the season, Bev Davis (below) helps deck the family's farm machinery for annual Parade of Lights. "A total of 11 families trim equipment in lights and such, then march around the area," she beams. "It's fun for everyone!"

Fiction

The Christmas Gift

By Betty Fulgham of Frankfort, Kentucky

"THIS will be the bestest Christmas ever," chirped tiny Dexie, the youngest in Kelly Dyer's class. Across the wood-paneled room, heads nodded in wide-eyed agreement.

It was a week before the holiday program, the biggest event of the year in the remote mountain community. Kelly tried to remain cheerful, but her misgivings were piling up faster than the snow outside the one-room school.

She'd tried to get the children to focus on costumes and props, but so far all they could think about was being on stage. Everyone knew their parts, but as the days went by without signs of anyone considering what to wear, well, she was sure it would be a disaster.

That was the last thing Kelly needed. This teaching position had been a lifesaver since her dad had taken sick. True, her brother had agreed to help out with the farm work, but they needed the income from her job to pay for spring planting.

What would she do if the superintendent thought

she couldn't put on a decent Christmas program? Nerves on edge, Kelly began to remind the kids about costumes.

Just then the door flew open, ushering in a well-bundled figure bearing brightly wrapped boxes. Mrs. Farquier from the Ladies Aid Society! Kelly'd forgotten all about the visit.

Every year, the women's group gathered clothing and small toys to give the children at Christmas. For some like Dexie, these would be the only gifts they'd receive. Spirits soared as new shoes, hats, shirts and skirts were quickly unwrapped.

Dexie stood in the midst of the group, working on her package. Impatiently, she tore away the last scrap of paper…and froze. Eyes wide, Dexie stared at the crimson coat with gold lining clutched in her hands. "Oh, look, Miss Kelly! This is the prettiest coat I ever saw," she exclaimed.

"My niece moved away before she could wear it," said Mrs. Farquier, watching Dexie twirl around.

The child's delight was contagious, and Kelly found herself enjoying the afternoon's program rehearsal. When she brought up costumes, however, only Dexie showed any interest at all.

"I'm bringing the star! I'm an angel and angels bring stars," the little girl proclaimed. "Big shiny ones!"

"Well," smiled Kelly, "at least we'll have a star."

The night of the play brought more snow, but that didn't stop anyone from attending. The school was soon brimming with people, including Mr. Carr, the superintendent.

Kelly tried to ignore

her dismay as the children arrived without costumes. Still, the play got underway smoothly.

When the reader got to the part about the Star in the East, Dexie tumbled off the stage. Concerned, Kelly hurried over to help…but before she could, up popped a tiny hand holding a big gold star stretched over a coat hanger.

"Here it is! Here's the star," cried Dexie as she scrambled back onto the platform. Ripples of laughter rolled through the room, and Kelly couldn't help but join in.

Bowing to thunderous applause, the children giggled and fidgeted, then ran to greet their families. Kelly nodded and smiled at a student as she bent to pick a program off the floor, almost colliding with the superintendent.

"Nice production, Miss Dyer," Mr. Carr beamed. "Clever idea to have no costumes this year! Teaches the children to be resourceful."

"Why, thank you, Mr. Carr. I…"

"Leave it to children to remind us what this season is all about. I'm looking forward to your next event," he added, moving quickly toward the door.

"So glad you could come," Kelly managed before he vanished into the snowy night.

Dexie appeared with her coat over her arm. "Merry Christmas, Miss Kelly," she grinned. "Aren't you glad my coat came in time for the star? I remembered not to be selfish with my things. An' I gave the very best gift I had, just like the three Wise Men did!"

Selfish with things? In time for the star? What did Dexie mean, Kelly wondered as she hurried to the door in time to see the family pile into their car, Dexie holding her coat despite the chill.

The moon came out from behind the clouds, shedding just enough light for Kelly to glimpse a large star-shaped hole in the gold lining of Dexie's coat.

"You're right, Mr. Carr," Kelly said softly as she watched Dexie's family drive away. "Sometimes it takes a little child to remind us what Christmas is all about." ☆

Live Nativity Makes Dramatic Statement About Yule Season

THE STARS in Oskaloosa, Iowa are extra-bright come December, Sue Van Hal says of her rural community. In fact, they keep the Christmas spirit shining all across the Midwest.

"Our congregation presents a live Nativity that goes beyond the season's hustle and bustle," Sue observes about the drive-through pageant she helps direct for the First Church of the Nazarene. "Some 5,000 visitors come to see it each year.

"We feature 12 scenes portraying the Nativity—from the road to Bethlehem…to a crowded inn…to the Holy Family at the manger. Church members become shepherds, angels and wise men in disguise—often involving three generations in one family.

"Guests drive through the Nativity set up in our parking lot, following a path lit by hundreds of white lights. A sign with a Scripture verse describes what each scene depicts."

As she prepares for the 20th annual pageant, Sue reports there are plenty of tales to tell besides the traditional Christmas story!

"One year, our flock of sheep escaped and caused quite a commotion until we got them rounded up," she recalls one wild and woolly adventure.

"Thanks to local farmers, we also spotlight horses, donkeys and chickens. Of course, the kids love the three camels we rent for the Magi."

By late summer, her church takes on a Christmas cast as Sue starts recruiting over 280 Nativity volunteers— her husband, Greg, daughter Kami, 9, and son Cory, 5, among them.

"Each scene is staffed by two sets of characters, alternating half-hour shifts, with a warm-up break in between," she explains.

"We've had temperatures below zero, so our actors often wear coats, mittens, scarves and boots under their costumes. We say the weather determines the 'heft' of our production."

The fact that the free seasonal show goes on is a cheerful miracle in itself, Sue attests. "Handy helpers, including my father, build, paint and assemble the scenery—from Joseph's carpenter shop to a humble stable. Talented ladies from the church stitch glittery angel costumes and kingly robes.

"Many families attend every December from as far away as Minneapolis, Omaha and Chicago. By trying to recreate the first Christmas, we're giving a special present to the public that anyone from age one to 90-plus can enjoy," Sue smiles.

Editor's Note: *The live Nativity will be held this year on December 13-15 from 6:30-8:30 p.m. Oskaloosa is about 60 miles southeast of Des Moines at the intersection of U.S. Highway 63*

SEASON'S REASON is played up in fine country style at outdoor pageant Sue Van Hal (in red shirt above) helps organize at church.

and state highways 92, 137 and 163.

For details, send a self-addressed stamped envelope to Sue at the First Church of the Nazarene, 1215 3rd Ave. E., Oskaloosa IA 52577 or phone 1-515/673-3417. ☆

Christmas Windows

Feathery wisps of snowflakes waft
Round haloed street lamp lights,
As church bells of the evening chime
To hail their Yuletide flight.
Down festive, snow-clad, cobbled streets
Come friends and families,
Admiring Christmas windows on
A merry Christmas Eve.

Caroling choirs of children lift
Their voices to extol
The coming of the One who dwells
In faithful hearts and souls.
And in trimmed shops on proud display
He's seen in reverent style—
A creche in Christmas windows lauds
This little Christmas Child.

In homes before a flickering hearth,
Good families gather round,
Where warmest Yuletide wishes ring,
Where peace on earth resounds.
And in that glowing firelight,
Eyes gleam in hearts so dear,
Like lustrous Christmas windows filled
With wondrous Christmas cheer.

—Lon Myruski
Washingtonville, New York

May the wondrous magic of Christmas fill your hearts and homes all throughout the year.

INDEX

 Share Your Holiday Joy!

DO *YOU* celebrate Christmas in a special way? If so, we'd like to know! We're already gathering material for our next *Country Woman Christmas* book. And we need your help!

Do you have a nostalgic holiday-related story to share? Perhaps you have penned a Christmas poem…or a heart-warming fiction story?

Does your family carry on a favorite holiday tradition? Or do you deck your halls in some festive way? Maybe you know of a Christmas-loving country woman others might like to meet?

We're looking for *original* Christmas quilt patterns and craft projects, too, plus homemade Nativities, gingerbread houses, etc. Don't forget to include your best recipes for holiday-favorite main-dish meats, home-baked cookies, candies, breads, etc.!

Send your ideas and photos to "*CW* Christmas Book", 5925 Country Lane, Greendale WI 53129. (Enclose a self-addressed stamped envelope if you'd like materials returned.) ☆